From Anger to Zion

From Anger to Zion

An Alphabet of Faith

PORTER TAYLOR

MOREHOUSE PUBLISHING
A Continuum imprint
HARRISBURG · LONDON · NEW YORK

Morehouse Publishing, P.O. Box 1321, Harrisburg, PA 17105
Morehouse Publishing, The Tower Building, 11 York Road, London SE1 7NX

Morehouse Publishing is a Continuum imprint.

Cover design: Lee Singer

Library of Congress Cataloging-in-Publication Data

Taylor, G. Porter.
  From anger to zion : an alphabet of faith / G. Porter Taylor.
    p. cm.
  ISBN 0-8192-2111-2 (pbk.)
  1. Episcopal Church—Sermons. 2. Anglican Communion—Sermons.
I. Title.
  BX5937.T29F76 2004
  252'.03—dc22

                              2004003659

Printed in the United States of America

04   05   06   07   08   09   10   9   8   7   6   5   4   3   2   1

To my parents,
Richard and Sarah Taylor

CONTENTS

ACKNOWLEDGMENTS

Because these essays first were sermons, I must express my gratitude to the people to whom they were preached. All sermons are conversations about things that matter. I am grateful to the people of St. Gregory the Great Episcopal Church in Athens, Georgia, for encouraging and participating in such conversations. Over and over, this community has gone deeper and deeper into the mysteries of faith.

I am thankful to Lee Ann Pingel for her enormous and generous help in the editing of this manuscript and to Hortense Bates, whose wonderful sense of order is a needed corrective to my incorrigible drive toward chaos. I am grateful to Conoly Hester for her help in proofreading the book. I also wish to express my appreciation to Debra Farrington for her encouragement and cheerful support.

I am also appreciative of the many writers, preachers, and speakers who have inspired me and from whom I have borrowed. I am especially grateful to Richard Rohr. I give him credit throughout this manuscript for his ideas and words that I have directly borrowed, but I am aware of how much of these essays grow out of his writings and teachings.

Most of all, I am grateful to my family: Arthur, my son; Marie, my daughter; and, as always, Jo, my wife.

ANGER

Be angry but do not sin; do not let the sun go down on
your anger.

—Ephesians 4:26

Let's admit it. Most of the time we don't know what to do with
anger—especially as Christians. We rarely applaud anger as a
virtue. You don't hear people saying, "He is such a good
Christian because he is so angry."

No, what we usually hear is, "He is such a good Christian
because he is so *nice*." We think being nice is a much better
trait than being angry. And, for those of us who are
Episcopalian, we might add "tasteful." We'll take nice and
tasteful over angry any day.

But guess what? In the Letter to the Ephesians, Paul explains
how to live as Christians. "Nice" and "tasteful" don't make the
list, but "anger" does. Paul says, "Be angry, but do not sin." No
doubt the Ephesians pricked up their ears at that! Suddenly this
Christianity thing took on a whole new perspective. Be angry,
but do not sin.

1

Anger is very tricky, a double-edged sword. It can be a vice or a virtue, depending on how it is used. There is no doubt that anger is dangerous; it is so explosive that we can easily slip from righteous anger into sinful anger. Consequently, we need to be prayerful and careful with our anger. We need to pay attention to the hallmarks of righteous and sinful anger.

Sinful Anger

Anger is energy, and energy must be transferred into activity. Anger comes from our passions, but it becomes sin when it is destructive, either to others or to ourselves. Pent-up anger will either explode uncontrollably or eat away at our hearts and souls until it takes up all of our interior space. Unless and until we deal with our anger, there is no room in us for anything else. As a result, we are incapable of action. For this reason, Paul cautions us not to let the sun go down on our anger.

Once I got angry with my wife, Jo, but being the nice, tasteful person that I am, I held it in. On the inside I was boiling, but on the outside, I was "fine." In the middle of the night, I had a nightmare that I was being suffocated, and to free myself from my attacker I screamed, "Get off of me!" and crashed my elbow into Jo's ribs. That was a hint that anger doesn't magically disappear; it will come out one way or another, and unless it's channeled constructively, it will almost certainly burst out destructively.

Thus, Paul also reminds us "we are members of one another." When we lash out at another, we do injury not only to that person but to ourselves as well. Whether we are angry at another over a truly unjust act or simply out of a selfish need to have things our way, the great temptation is to feel superior to the other person. Our anger helps us tower over the other person and, like Zeus, send down our thunderbolts. Venting our emotions this way may make us feel good, but it's destructive. Regardless of the cause, rage or vengeance is not righteous anger.

Righteous Anger

Anger is connected with our values: we only get angry about things we care about. I don't trust anyone who never gets angry, because that person has no passions. Who would just shrug off seeing two men push an elderly lady down to steal her purse? We get angry when we see something wrong. Moses was angry when he came down Mount Sinai and saw the golden calf. Jesus was angry when he saw the moneychangers in the Temple. Jesus was even angry enough with the Pharisees and the scribes to call them names—a "brood of vipers" (Matthew 3:7).

The key to dealing well with anger is provided at the start of Ephesians 5: "Therefore be imitators of God." We are to be angry, but we are to imitate God's anger. God does get angry, but not over traffic jams or bad calls by referees. God is angry when humankind does not conform its ways to God's ways. God is angry when we do not live moral lives: when we do not do justice, love kindness, and walk humbly with our God (Micah 6:8). God gets angry because God longs for us to be our best, as individuals and as a people, but we settle for so little. Why *not* have a world of justice and mercy and peace? In other words, let's get angry over something worthwhile. It is when we find ourselves irate over traffic or sports that we should heed Paul's instruction to "put away from you all bitterness and wrath and anger and wrangling and slander, together with all malice" (Ephesians 4:31). Righteous anger is reserved for the deep sinfulness of our world and its structures that perpetuate injustice.

When we are angry over appropriate issues, our anger should imitate God's anger. When God gets angry, God enters into a dialogue (albeit a heated one) with the people. God says, "You have not followed my laws. You have sinned," and the people of God argue back. However, the relationship is maintained: the whole point of the dialogue is to reestablish the covenant.

God's anger always leads to a new covenant; it always serves a larger purpose. Even the flood in Genesis—an example of

God's anger at its most extreme—led to reconciliation between God and humankind. God was so angry with the people who would not walk in God's ways that in a fit of anger God destroyed them. However, out of this came a new and everlasting promise that God's anger would never be destructive again. The Hebrew Bible is filled with this pattern of anger/conversation/new covenant.

It is this new covenant, this disruption of the status quo, that makes anger—ours or God's—so scary. But the truth is that most of the time the status quo needs disruption. We need to be angry the way Hosea and Amos and Jeremiah and John the Baptist and Jesus were angry. We need to be angry the way Mothers Against Drunk Driving are MADD. Our anger is the force that can make our world accountable and move us to talk about how our ways fall short of God's ways. Then, when that talk is finished, we need to have the courage to reach out to the other person and establish a new covenant. We need to disrupt the status quo, and then we need to have the wisdom to make something new.

So let's not waste our time and our passion being angry over not getting our way; let's not waste our time and our passion screaming at the traffic or at soccer referees. Instead, let's think about the world God wants. When we see how far we are from that, let's be angry, but instead of sinning, let's imitate God.

B

BLESSED

Blessed are the poor in spirit, for theirs is the kingdom of heaven.

—Matthew 5:3

In February 1985, I went on a week's retreat to a Carmelite monastery in Crestone, Colorado. The plane landed in Denver at about two in the afternoon, and I rented a car. I drove south for about an hour and then came to a roadblock: the wind was blowing so much snow across the road that it had to be closed, and the patrolman could not tell me how long the delay would be.

Patience has never been my strong suit. So, as the cars with Colorado tags lined up to wait, I whipped out my map and figured out an alternate route: back to Denver and then east and south. I would just circle the blowing snow. However, I later came to understand that there was a reason those Colorado cars waited patiently in line. I did make it to Crestone, but it was midnight and it was snowing.

Now, Crestone is a very tiny town, and at night, it was pitch black. There were no signs saying MONASTERY THIS WAY; there was no tourism office or welcome station, and they wouldn't have been open at midnight, anyway. At one point I saw a driveway that looked like it might lead to a monastery, but after two hundred yards I realized I was lost. And that it was snowing. And cold. And dark. I backed carefully out of the drive and started driving around more or less aimlessly. After a while, I turned a corner and saw a house blazing with lights. A family was sitting around the kitchen table. I went to the door and knocked, and when someone came, I said, "I'm lost. Can you help?"

Jesus begins the Sermon on the Mount by proclaiming: "Blessed are the poor in spirit, for theirs is the kingdom of heaven." Jesus telescopes the whole sermon into that one sentence. In fact, the rest of the Sermon on the Mount is a way of explaining that sentence. To be "blessed" is to be "happy" or "fortunate."

In Luke's version of the sermon, Jesus says, "Blessed are the poor" and then follows with "Woe to the rich." But Matthew's version is different. According to Matthew, Jesus says, "Blessed are the *poor in spirit*." What does that mean?

We need to distinguish between the spiritually poor and the poor in spirit.[1] The spiritually poor are those who are stuck in a place cut off from God and grace. To be spiritually poor is to have "poor, narrow thoughts, starved hopes . . . a hard, love-less heart, a life without a vision of God, and without peace."[2] There is nothing happy or fortunate or blessed about being spiritually poor.

To be spiritually poor is to be alone, and that is one way of being in hell. The life of the spiritually poor becomes completely self-referential: whatever they do, whatever they say, it's always,

---

1. Percy C. Ainsworth, "The Kingdom of the Poor," in *Weavings* (January/February 2000), 29–34.

2. Ibid., 32.

"Me, me, me, me." There is so much "me" that there is no room for the Spirit. As a wise woman once said to me, "People can't get enough of what they don't need." That's the vicious cycle of being spiritually poor: I don't feel good about myself, so I inflate my ego. That alienates more people, so I feel worse about myself, and the cycle starts all over again.

The difference between the spiritually poor and the poor in spirit is this: the poor in spirit are blessed because they know they are poor, and they know they are poor because they know they are human—made from earth, limited, and sinful. The spiritually poor are stuck and in despair, but the poor in spirit turn, in their poverty, to God, and so they have hope.

But let's face it—neither "blessed are the poor in spirit" nor any of the other beatitudes make any sense to self-sufficient America. They make no sense to the spiritually poor. Jesus is proclaiming the upside-down Good News: the last are first, losing is finding, poverty is riches, and *spiritual wealth is based on need*. Happy are those who know their need for God, because they will ask; and because they ask, they will receive.

"I am lost. Can you help?"

I didn't know it at the time, but asking for help is the doorway to blessedness, because the point where we meet our limitations is the place where we meet God. If we can do everything, if we can buy everything we need, if we can manufacture a life without any unpleasant events ever happening, then why do we need God?

The poor in spirit are blessed because they have no illusions about their need and can receive grace with open arms. I read once that when Carl Jung was an old man, one of his admirers asked him, "What has your pilgrimage really been?" Jung replied, "My journey has consisted of climbing down 10,000 ladders, until now, at the end of my life, I can extend the hand of friendship to this little clod of earth that I am."

To extend the hand of friendship to the little clod of earth that is each of us is to be poor in spirit and it is to be blessed, because we know we are limited but not alone. We know that our lives are not ours because we belong to God. We don't have to work everything out; we just have to participate in what God is working out. We don't have to know all the answers; we just have to say, "I'm lost, God. Can you help?"

The family in Crestone gave me directions. It turned out I had wandered to the wrong side of town. So, I retraced my steps (which always puts us on the Way), and as I turned a corner, I saw lights down the side of the mountain. I crunched through the snow and rang the bell, and when a monk opened the door, I asked, "Is this where I belong?"

He smiled and said, "Welcome. We've been waiting for you." In that moment, far from home, looking out over the snowy dark, I knew that I was blessed.

BODY

Look at my hands and my feet; see that it is I myself. Touch me and see.

—Luke 24:39

They heard the stories, but after all, stories are just stories. Thomas said he touched his hands. Mary Magdalene said she grabbed his feet. Cleopas said he ate dinner with him. Peter said he ate breakfast with him. But, as they say, talk is cheap.

So when he appeared among them, they didn't know what to think. Is it really him? How could it be? He's dead. It's only our imagination. We just feel his Spirit. No, it's a ghost; it's an apparition. Call Shirley MacLaine. Call Bishop Pike. Call Edgar Cayce. They'll know how it works.

The risen Christ stands among them and challenges all their assumptions. He says, "Look at me. I am not a ghost. I am Jesus. Prove it to yourselves. Give me something to eat." When they did, they didn't give him angel food cake. They gave him a big hunk of cooked fish, something substantial like southern-fried catfish—something a body with solid teeth can bite into.

The bodily resurrection always generates conversation, which is well and good. It's always refreshing to hear folks talk about scripture. However, often the conversation gets located in the wrong place. We want to know how it could happen instead of what it means. I don't think the how question is the crucial one. After all, the point is that the resurrection is new. That's why it's such a big deal. If we could explain it, we wouldn't need it.

I cannot explain the physical resurrection of Jesus, and I am not very interested in doing that anyway. However, I am very interested in what Jesus' bodily resurrection means for the disciples and for Christians ever since and especially for you and me. Because we say the Nicene Creed in churches Sunday after Sunday, we aren't directly confronted with this issue on a weekly basis. That creed says, "We believe in the resurrection of the dead." However, the Apostles' Creed says something different: "We believe in the resurrection of the body."

Saying "the resurrection of the body" affirms our belief in resurrection and not in mere immortality. If Jesus is a ghost, then the physical world can be split from the spiritual world and we can and will value the spiritual over the physical. If the risen Jesus is a ghost, then we can believe in an immortal soul that is separate from and superior to our bodies. Our bodies die, but our souls go to heaven and live forever. Those who believe this believe that the essence of Jesus doesn't die on the cross, but escapes his body. Therefore, the disciples experience that immortal essence we call his soul.

That's a nice idea and many religions believe it. But it's not Christian. Christianity at its best has always asserted that the body and soul are inextricably connected. When Jesus died, all of him died: body and soul. When he was resurrected, all of him was resurrected. I think that's why the risen Jesus asks for something to eat. Surely he's not hungry; he just polished off bread and wine in Emmaus. He is reminding the disciples that he is not a ghost and that he is not an angel. Angels and ghosts don't eat food and they don't have bodies—and they don't die.

Christianity is a religion of the body and the soul all wrapped up together. That's what the Incarnation is all about. The Word became flesh and dwells among us. The intangible Logos became completely body and experienced what bodies feel: hunger and exhaustion and pain and death. If Jesus is just a ghost, then the resurrection is not about the body and not about the world. Then we are right back with the gnostics, who claim that we can split soul and body and we can value one and ignore or degrade the other.

This split between body and soul always plagues our culture. One extreme is to worship the body without any sense of the soul or of God's resurrection. So we have a world of addictions—addictions to stimulation and sensation. We do anything to feel something. Another alternative is our addiction to our self-image. How I look is who I am.

The other extreme is the worship of the soul and the deathly fear of the body and our senses. We cut ourselves off from the physical, both our bodies and the earth. This may be why Christianity has such a long history of making people ashamed of their bodies. In like manner, instead of being connected to the material world, we have instead claimed dominion over it. We look at the natural order as only a resource for our ends instead of being part of God's creation. No wonder we now face ecological disaster.

If Jesus is just a ghost, then soul and body are not forever linked. Then the resurrection is not a new creation but only an escape of the soul from the trap of the body. But as Christians, we proclaim something else. We believe in the resurrection of the body. Even if we don't say it week after week, we ought to know it. After all, each of our sacraments involves the body. They all involve the senses because, through the sacraments, the whole self is transformed: soul and body. We eat the bread; we drink the wine. The bishop puts her hands on your heads at

Confirmation and Ordination. The wedding couple hold hands and say their vows. The holy oil is placed on our heads at Confession and during the Last Rites. If the water doesn't touch your body, you aren't baptized.

Sacraments are outward visible signs of inward and spiritual grace given by Christ as sure and certain means by which we receive that grace. The body is the means of grace. Touch and see. Do you have something to eat?

That means this world has value and is part of God's salvation. This world is not something we endure so our souls can be freed from our bodies to live in some heavenly realm. Soul and body, spirit and matter are inseparably connected. Resurrection is raising all of us, soul and body, to new life.

God isn't rescuing souls from the corrupt earth; God is transforming, resurrecting, all of creation: soul and body. That means this world is important and how we treat one another's bodies is important. How we relate to the physical world is important. Therefore, it matters that people have enough to eat. It matters that we can enjoy the sheer goodness of creation. It matters that all people have access to medical care so that they can treat their bodies with respect.

The resurrection is not just a one-time event after our deaths. It is ongoing. The resurrection of the body doesn't just comfort us with the knowledge that we will see Aunt Jane in heaven. Instead, it means we can experience that transformation as we are engaged in this bodily world here and now. Why else do you think Jesus took so much time to heal people's bodies? Why else is he eating all the time? It's because the redemption of souls and the redemption of the body are one.

The resurrected Christ stood among them and said "touch and see." That touch was resurrection, and that touch has been passed body and soul through the ages from one body and soul to the next so that God's people would know that it's one world.

Now it's our turn. One ordinary day he will stand among us and say, "I am resurrecting this world—body and soul. Touch and see."

CALLING

I appointed you a prophet to the nations.

—Jeremiah 1:5

The day it happened was a homecoming because the words came into his heart from somewhere outside yet seemed absolutely familiar. It was as if he heard his own voice for the first time. He touched his mouth to see if he had spoken. In that moment, he could see. The confusion that so often clouded his world lifted. So often he had wondered, *Will we get the Assyrians off our backs for good? Can we trust the Babylonians? Are we going to be free? Does God want us to go to the Temple day after day to worship or is there another way?*

He wondered about these things. In fact, he thought more about these things than he did about getting on with his life. Everyone said it was time to think about following in his father's footsteps. It was time to think about marriage, a home, a normal life. But he thought about Judah and faithfulness and oppression.

So when the voice came inside him, at first he didn't know what it was: *"Jeremiah.* Go and deliver." He looked around, hoping there was another Jeremiah. *Who me? I'm fourteen years old. I'm a freshman in high school. I don't even have a license. Go where? Deliver whom?*

Even as he said it, he knew. He had always known somewhere in his heart that he was meant for this kind of service. He was just scared and he didn't want to look foolish. Every time he had heard some little voice saying his name, he had brushed it off. He told himself, *It's just my imagination. Maybe it's something I ate.* But this time it was too loud. This time he felt someone touch his mouth and it burned. That touch ran all the way through him, and Jeremiah knew that he wasn't alone. He knew that God was with him, and although he did not know where he was going, he was ready to go.

It's a nice story, isn't it? And it must be true because it's in the Bible, but what about us? Are we called or is that just for the Bible folks? If we are, what does it mean? What happens when you are called?

Well, the first thing is you never feel adequate. It's an automatic reaction. Jeremiah says, "I am only a boy." Moses says, "I can't talk very well." Isaiah says, "I am not holy enough." When God calls us, our first response is always "Not me. You got the wrong person. Whatever you need, I don't have it." Up to a point—and the point is where we give in and say, "Okay, I'll go anyway"—up to a point our reservations are actually healthy, because they force us to focus on what God is doing and not on what we are capable of doing. Jeremiah looked at Judah, who had been captive to the Assyrians forever, and he could not image how he—only a boy—could do much about his country's plight. Moses looked at the Israelites, captive to Egypt, and he could not imagine how he could do much. However, in a strange sort of way, the sign of being called is this sense of inadequacy.

If someone comes up to you and says, "God has called me to save the world and I am completely prepared to do it," run, because that is a clear sign the person is not called. In *The Lord of the Rings*, those people who think they are the best person to carry the ring are exactly the ones you don't want anywhere near so much power. Instead, the one who is chosen is the small hobbit, who only says, "I will take the ring, though I do not know the way." *We* do not know the way, but we don't need to so long as we are connected to the One who *is* the Way.

Of course, Jeremiah doesn't know how to bring Judah back into righteousness, but God isn't asking him to know. God is asking him to participate in what God is doing; Jeremiah goes not because he knows what to say, but because God assures him that God will put the words into his mouth.

Yes, we are hesitant; yes, we do resist, but we go because in going we become more of who we are. God tells Jeremiah, "before you were born I consecrated you; I appointed you a prophet to the nations" (Jeremiah 1:5). Our calling is not so much about what we do; it's about who we are. One day we hear a voice deep within and we remember what we were born for because that voice within us beckons us to step out. At first, we don't know what the voice is, but if we listen, it's our voice saying our name. If we listen, our voice has the echo of God's voice and we know if we do not follow, we will never be completely alive.

Somewhere in his soul, Jeremiah has always known he is a prophet. Because there is no market for prophets, he hasn't listened to that voice. Of course, in his heart, he knows his deafness makes him a little less alive. Every time he looks at the Assyrians, he knows in his heart that he should speak out. Every time he looks at his fellow Israelites, part of him dies as he stays silent.

Each of us is called to follow that voice within that beckons us to manifest as who we are; that voice is actually our meeting place with God. There is a great joy in following God's call— because, for the first time in our lives, we fit. If you are a painter and you have embraced your calling, you'd paint for free. As a matter of fact, you probably do paint for free. It's who you are.

As the poet William Stafford writes, "Some time when the river is ice ask me / mistakes I have made. Ask me whether / what I have done is my life. . . ." He means that the greatest mistake is to live what is not your life.

Jeremiah feels inadequate, then he embraces that voice as his own, and finally he is called to go out on behalf of God. Isn't it amazing that no one in the Bible is called to go shopping or go to Super Bowl parties? God doesn't call us to serve ourselves. We are called to play our part in what God is doing; we are called to serve in the transformation of the world. Jeremiah is given power to pluck up and to pull down, to build and to plant, because it's God's plan to pluck up, pull down, to build and plant. When our inner calling is true, it is always matched by service to the world. Frederick Buechner has a wonderful definition of vocation: "The place God calls you to is the place where your deep gladness and the world's deep hunger meet."[1]

However, following your call by going into the world is always hard. The world is not really excited about being plucked up or pulled down. Many people did not want to hear Jeremiah or Amos or Jesus or St. Francis or Dorothy Day or Martin Luther King Jr. In like manner, many people were not excited when Pablo Picasso gave his first exhibit, and many were not excited when William Faulkner published *The Sound and the Fury*, either.

Many people will not be excited about your call, either. They'll say to you, "You're just a girl; you're not ready; it won't work."

When that happens, remember the best part of the call. Every time you step out to follow that inner voice, God whispers in your ear: "I am with you; I am with you; I am with you."

---

1. Frederick Buechner, *Wishful Thinking* (New York: HarperSanFrancisco, 1993), 119.

CHILD

Whoever welcomes one such child in my name welcomes me.

—Mark 9:37

When Robert was in high school, the world was in his hip
pocket. He started on the soccer team. He played guitar in a
rock band. He scored 1530 on the SATs. Not too many people
were surprised when he got into a prestigious university.
Clearly he was headed for great things. People said, "Remember
that boy's name because he is going places."

He went to college and did fine his first semester. But then,
in the spring, something happened. The dean of students called
his mother and said, "Your son hasn't been to any of his classes
in a month. Something could be wrong." However, they hadn't
actually seen him. No one had actually seen him. He had stayed
in his apartment for weeks. It turns out that at nineteen he had
a schizophrenic break.

So he moved back home and tried to hold down a job. But
it was hard. He talked to himself. He wouldn't bathe. He seldom changed his clothes. The young man who had the world
in his hip pocket now couldn't keep a job taking care of the
carts at the grocery store.

Here's the point. In less than a year, he had become invisi-
ble. Now when he walked down the street, people looked the
other way. No one was mean; no one said anything to him. No
one said anything to him because he no longer fit into the
power structure. He was no longer worth knowing. He had
gone from being somebody to being nobody in four months.

It is so easy for us to misunderstand the radical, upside-
down gospel. However, this isn't a new problem. Throughout
the gospels, Jesus teaches the disciples about the cross and his
future suffering. He warns them that to follow him means to

take up their own cross. Yet, their response is to get into an argument about who is the greatest. Clearly, they are clueless.

Jesus must know that words are not going to bring the point home. He can talk until he is blue in the face and they will still be asking who can sit at his right hand in heaven. So he shows them. He takes a child in his arms and declares, "Whoever receives one such child in my name receives God."

You know who it was he embraced, don't you? It wasn't the Gerber baby. It wasn't a Harry Potter look-alike. It was Robert. It was the boy everyone overlooked.

When we hear of Jesus taking a child into his arms, we make the story too cute for our own good. We think it's about Jesus telling his disciples not to be too worldly but to preserve their childhood innocence. That's nice and in other places he does say that. But not here.

In Jesus' day and time, people looked at children very differently than in ours. There, a child had virtually no status. A son didn't officially have his birthrights until he reached maturity. If a famine came into the land, children would be fed last after the adults. In the case of a fire, children would be rescued last after adults. In part, this was because of the high infant mortality rates: 30 percent of infants died in childbirth and 60 percent of children died before turning sixteen. Children were barely seen and never heard until they reached adulthood.

However, Jesus is saying to the disciples, "If you want to see God, stop looking at yourselves and your own reputations. Instead, look at those you overlook; look at the ones who cannot help your career, the ones who cannot build up your reputation. The ones who have nothing but their sheer humanity to offer. When you embrace them in my name, you will embrace me."

Until we realize this, it's all just ego. It's all just the way of the world. We are chasing after what New Testament scholar Marcus Borg calls the three As: achievements, affluence, appearance. What have you done? What do you own? How do you look? The radical good news of the gospel is that the world doesn't revolve around our egos. The world of grace is not about what we can do or what we own or how we look. It's about the gifts that God is always trying to give us if we will let go of our clutch on life so we can receive.

Richard Rohr, a Franciscan and founder of the Center for Action and Contemplation, says that we mistakenly assume that discipleship is the way of addition: one more achievement, one more experience, one more book or retreat or sermon. To our shock, discipleship is what he calls the "spirituality of subtraction." To be a disciple we must become aware of our enormous need for Jesus. Otherwise, why would we be willing to follow him to the cross? The disciples argue about who is the greatest because they are still trying to prove their worthiness. They are still promoting their own egos.

The good news of Jesus always sounds upside down to the world. The world never knows what to do with the spirituality of subtraction. To our great surprise, it's our wounds that save us, because they show us our enormous need of God's grace. As St. Paul says, "Therefore I am content with weaknesses, insults, hardships, persecutions, and calamities for the sake of Christ; for whenever I am weak, then I am strong" (2 Corinthians 12:10).

All we have to proclaim is the grace of God and the love of Jesus. That's all. It's not about our achievements or affluence or appearance. It's not about us at all. It's about the grace of God and the love of Jesus. The children of Jesus' day and of our day know that. Robert knows that. He isn't cutting a deal. He doesn't have an angle. He lacks any agenda but getting through the day.

You know what? If you can open your eyes and see him not as a lost twenty-four-year-old with wrinkled clothes and confused eyes, but if you can see him as Robert—simply Robert, a person just like you; one of God's children, just like you; a human being with a name and feelings and words worth hearing—if you can see him that way, you'll see the face of Jesus.

I know it's true. The last time I saw Robert, he shook my hand and said, "I am so glad to see you." And he was. But I heard him say, "I am so glad you came to see me." You know what? I was glad too. I was very glad, because seeing him opened a door in my heart that led to a land called grace.

CHURCH

> The gifts he gave were . . . to equip the saints for the work
> of ministry, for building up the body of Christ.
>
> —Ephesians 4:11–12

The Christians of Ephesus aren't sure what they have gotten themselves into. They accept all the creeds; they affirm the dogma; they know the stories about Jesus' miracles and death and resurrection. They like the breaking of bread and the sharing of the cup, and they've been baptized. They've signed on the dotted line, but there's still one question left: What does it mean to be the Church?

The news Paul has to tell them is not the news they expect to hear. Being the Church is not just about being orthodox or accepting dogma; it's not just about what you believe. Rather, being the Church has a lot to do with how you behave and how you believe.

Christianity is not merely a confession of belief. We are not Christians only because the teachings of Christ make sense. We are Christians because we have been grasped by the love of Jesus Christ, and that radical love has changed, is changing, and will continue to change us, not just in our ways of thinking, but in our ways of doing. We are Christians according to how we act as well as according to what we believe. That's one of the reasons we gather together as the Church: we come together to experience again Jesus' love in community, which is the hardest and yet the most authentic way of experiencing it. We discover Christ as the in-between, connecting us to one another in a holy communion.

The surprise for the Christians in Ephesus is not that they are now followers of Jesus Christ; the surprise is that they are now part of the body of Christ, and they are not exactly sure what that means, what being the Church means. Therefore, Paul is teaching them how to look at their lives differently. Instead of the virtues celebrated by society, like being right and powerful and superior, Paul offers a totally different set of virtues, like being humble and gentle and patient.

Paul tells the Christians in Ephesus that their task is not to be the most orthodox or the most righteous or the most pure; their task is to equip the saints for ministry and for building up the body of Christ.

When we think of "equipping," we think of obtaining equipment, as in gathering tents and sleeping bags and food for a camping trip. But the task Paul is addressing concerns how we relate to one another. The Greek word translated as "equip" means "to adjust thoroughly," as in putting a bone or part of the body into right relation with the other parts. So to equip the saints for ministry is like taking the whole congregation to the chiropractor for an adjustment. It is to get all the pieces functioning so that the blood flows well. The Good News of Jesus Christ is not just something we proclaim, it's something we experience with one another. Grace and forgiveness and communion are not concepts, not ideas to present; they are realities that happen between people. We equip one another as we align our will with God's will, as we make sure we work together smoothly for God's purposes. Paul tells the Ephesians, "You cannot proclaim to others what you do not experience yourselves," and this Church—with its strange mix of people— is the place to experience what is preached.

Of course, this is not easy—especially since the Church doesn't work like those reality television shows where cast members vote each other off the show: instead of voting people out, we keep inviting them in. It's been that way from the beginning. The

Gentile Christians in Ephesus asked Paul, "You mean we are part of the same Church as those Jews? If we have to sit next to *them*, all we'll do is argue over circumcision or food . . . and we don't like the way those other converts act, either. They're so loud and they wave their hands around in the air when they worship. Paul, what about those folks from the south side of town? We don't like their politics, and we don't want to associate with them."

So, Paul has to lay it out again. "Look," he says, "we are all in this boat together. It's not about being right, it's about growing up together and bearing with one another in love. It's about humility, gentleness, patience."

Some years ago my wife and I were in Chapel Hill, meeting with a friend who is a religion professor. He asked me about being a priest, and I started complaining about all the divisive parties in the Episcopal Church. I complained about how the liberals and conservatives couldn't get along and moaned about all the fighting over the controversial issues. Finally, when I paused for breath, he looked at me and said, "Well, you know, churches are places for people to learn to love."

And so they are, yet how hard it is. The Church is the place where we must be humble and gentle and patient with one another and let the love of Jesus Christ enable us to love one another.

Paul tells the Ephesians that they are to "grow up in every way" into Christ, but growing up takes time. It means hanging in there with one another, holding our tongues when we want to say "I told you so," being patient as we watch our brothers and sisters bash around in the dark. It means not giving up on each other, not walking away from one another. We act this way not just for others but also for ourselves: we are all learning how to be a community together. We are learning that the only glue that will bind us together is the love of Jesus Christ and that the only way to be humble and gentle and patient with each other is by remembering that God is in control.

Therefore, our job is to see what God is doing in this place and then to equip ourselves, to align ourselves with that divine activity. We don't have to make it happen; we only have to participate in what is happening.

We need to remember that Jesus wasn't too picky about who came to him. That's why he gave the Pharisees such fits. The Pharisees thought that if you touched the wrong people, you'd get religious cooties. If someone had bad eating practices or bad politics or came from the bad side of the tracks, you'd better keep your distance if you wanted to stay pure. But, as we see in the feeding of the five thousand, Jesus says that we all eat together and we all share a common cup. It's only together that we experience a holy communion.

A story is told of the Desert Fathers that a group of the monks came to the abbot very distressed because one of the new monks was sleeping during the prayers. The monks complained that it ruined the service for them and set a bad example. They said he was breaking the rules of the order and ought to be punished or even dismissed. Finally, when their complaining was done and they asked the abbot what he would do, the abbot said, "Actually if I saw a brother sleeping, I would put his head on my knees and let him rest."[2]

Humility. Gentleness. Patience. For, after all, churches are places to learn to love.

CLEAN AND UNCLEAN

A leper came to him begging him, and kneeling he said to him, "If you choose, you can make me clean."

—Mark 1:40

---

2. In *Stories of the Spirit, Stories of the Heart*, ed. Christina Feldman and Jack Kornfield (New York: HarperCollins, 1991), 169.

In order to realize what's going on in the encounter of Jesus and the leper, we need to know about leprosy and we need to know a little Greek. Today, we think of leprosy as Hansen's disease, a contagious, degenerative skin disorder. The people of Jesus' time had a much broader definition, however. For them, leprosy was a not so much a disease as a broad category of ritual impurity. The Holiness Code forbade many acts and conditions, but it especially forbade those conditions that mixed unlike elements. For example, it was taboo to plant two kinds of grain in one field, or to wear garments made of two kinds of cloth, or to interbreed two kinds of cattle, or even to yoke two kinds of animals. Leprosy, therefore, violated a taboo by causing two skin colors, and if a person's skin was not pure, then the person was not pure. Blotches on one's skin indicated blotches on one's soul. One could be declared a leper for having a birthmark, or psoriasis, or ringworm, or any ailment that changed one's skin color. In fact, there is some indication that, ironically enough, if a person had such a severe case of leprosy that he or she had only one skin color again, the person could be declared clean.

The Old Testament is clear about how lepers are to be treated. We read in Leviticus that "the person who has the leprous disease shall wear torn clothes and let the hair of his head be disheveled; and he shall cover his upper lip and cry out, 'Unclean, unclean.' . . . He shall live alone; his dwelling shall be outside the camp" (13:45–46).

With this in mind, let's look at the story from Mark. The leper comes to Jesus and says, "If you choose, you can make me clean." The leper knows that Jesus has the power to bring the outcast back into the circle of community. "If you choose, you can see me not as a pariah, not as someone to live apart, not as someone doomed to cry 'Unclean' for his entire life . . . but as one of you." Jesus responds by taking three actions, actions that tell us about our own ministry: connection, reorientation, and reconfiguration.

Connection

"Moved with pity, Jesus stretched out his hand and touched him" (Mark 1:41). This touch is neither a metaphor nor just a gesture. Jesus makes contact with the man who is unclean and thereby risks being made unclean himself. According to the law, touching a leper meant he *became* a leper until he could go to the Temple and be purified.

Touch always involves risk, because it signifies that your life is now part of my life; I am broadening my circle to include you. Americans think of ourselves as a very accepting culture, but we have confused connection with toleration. We casually say, "I have no problem with lepers. Live and let live is my motto." We do not, however, share our lives with the lepers. We never risk incorporating them into our circle. Instead, we simply ignore them.

Jesus does not say to the leper, "It's okay with me if you live that way, so long as you keep your distance." He doesn't *tolerate* the leper, he *touches* him. Toleration will never heal anyone; it's just a way of avoiding either confrontation or connection. Jesus is calling for us to do more than maintain our purity while we keep the other person at arm's length. He is calling for us to touch the person, to make a connection, even if it threatens our sense of identity.

I started reading an amazing book called *Autobiography of a Face* by Lucy Grealy. At age nine, Lucy Grealy was diagnosed with cancer and had to have one-third of her jaw removed.

She writes, "I spent five years of my life being treated for cancer, but since then I've spent fifteen years being treated for nothing other than looking different from everyone else. It was the pain from . . . feeling ugly that I always viewed as the great tragedy of my life. The fact that I had cancer seemed minor in comparison."[3]

---

3. Lucy Grealy, *Autobiography of a Face* (Boston: Houghton Mifflin, 1994), jacket.

Lucy repeatedly asks her acquaintances to choose to make
her clean, but none so choose. The tragedy of this book is that
no one touches Lucy during her childhood and youth; everyone in her life is content to let her wander around in her leper
status. Her days are so filled with ridicule and neglect that her
only relief is time spent with horses. In the horses' presence,
"nothing else mattered. . . . Horses neither disapproved nor
approved of what I looked like. . . ."[4] Lucy loves the touch, the
connection between herself and the horse. She loves to lie on
the back of one particular horse as he wanders in the field—
feeling held, feeling as if she belongs in the world, feeling
touched and clean.

Reorientation

"'I do choose,' Jesus said. 'Be clean!' Immediately the leprosy
left him and he was cured." Once we make connection with
someone, we see him or her in a new light. We see everything
in a new light. Our understanding of purity is shaken, and we
must reorient ourselves. Whenever we connect with someone,
our lives are changed. "I do choose" means that we have the
courage to act upon that change by changing the way we see, by
reorienting ourselves. We are no longer captives of our society's
categories or purity code.

We are all blind in one way or another; we all have pre-
judged people to some extent, and see in the other person what
we expect to see. Expanding our vision requires an act of will:
unless we make an effort to remove our filters, we will always
see another person less than clearly. Ask yourself, "Who is it
that I cannot see as a child of God? Whom have I placed outside the circle of those I deem worthy?"

Of course, there are the obvious categories of race and class
and nationality and sexual orientation that may tempt us to

---

4. Ibid., 152.

prejudge. But we make people into lepers in more subtle ways, as well: What are your politics? What degrees do you have? What teams do you root for? What church do you go to? What foods do you eat? Once I asked a friend, an ardent Republican, "What do you do about your politics when you talk to your friends who are Democrats?" She said, "It's easy. I don't have any friends who are Democrats."

"If you choose, you can make me clean." We must find ways to say, "I do choose." There is a moment of decision in *Huckleberry Finn* that shows how we are able to choose. Huck is torn between his sense of society's regulations and his conscience. He has written Miss Watson a letter telling her where Jim is so that she can have him captured and brought back to be a slave once more. But Huck keeps thinking of the times Jim's life has touched his own; he keeps thinking of Jim—not in the category of leper or slave, but just as Jim—until finally Huck risks the penalty from his society. He says, "All right then, I'll go to hell," and tears the letter up.[5] Touch changes us.

Reconfiguration

"[Jesus] sent him away at once, saying to him, 'See that you say nothing to anyone; but go, show yourself to the priest'" (1:43–44). This is where our knowing a little Greek helps. There is another way to translate this passage: "With a snort of indignation, Jesus sent him away at once." Similarly, there is a different but equally correct way to translate "moved with compassion" in verse 41: "Moved by anger, Jesus stretched out his hand and touched the man." Jesus is not angry at the man; he is angry at the Temple and the priests.[6] He is angry at the institution which, in the name of God, does not do God's will

---

5. Samuel Clemens, *The Adventures of Huckleberry Finn* (New York: Norton, 1962), 168.

6. Ched Myers, *Binding the Strong Man* (Maryknoll: Orbis, 1992), 153.

because it cannot let go of its neat categories of who is clean and who is unclean. There is a reason this episode happens in the country, away from Jerusalem and the Temple. All institutions—including the Church—create lepers. Every time we label some people as "in," we label others as "out."

I had a seminary professor who was fond of saying, "Christianity is a grand idea. It's too bad we've never tried it." He meant that we always fall short of God's vision of the body of Christ: the holy communion of God's people connected to one another as they are connected to Christ.

Therefore, once we have been touched—once we have chosen to change the way we see—Jesus sends us, like the leper, back to the institution in an effort to broaden its boundaries. We are to tell one another that maybe it's okay to plant two grains in one field; maybe it's okay to wear garments of two kinds of cloth; maybe it's okay to let lepers into our church and into our lives.

No doubt we would prefer our world to be a pure place with neat categories and clear distinctions between clean and unclean, but God is inviting us to a different adventure of faith—an adventure of connection, reorientation, and reconfiguration. God is inviting us to an encounter away from the Temple and our clearly ordered ideas. God is inviting us to touch real people that we usually overlook, then to choose to invite them into our circle because God knows that is how we, and the Church, and the world are changed.

CROSS

> If any want to become my followers, let them deny themselves and take up their cross and follow me.
>
> —Matthew 16:24

Clearly, Jesus does not know how to market a product. Words like "deny" and "cross" never sell.

Why not try, "If any want to become my followers, let them be assured that they will be safe and successful and secure"? It's no wonder the cross is a stumbling block. However, like it or not, if we are to follow Jesus, we will have to take up our crosses.

The cross is the doorway to new life: resurrected life, the life of grace and freedom. It is always a hard door to enter. No wonder Peter says to Jesus, "God forbid it, Lord! This must never happen to you" (Matthew 16:22). And, we would echo, "This must never happen to us!" We want what theologian Dietrich Bonhoeffer called "cheap grace." He wrote, "Cheap grace is the preaching of forgiveness without requiring repentance . . . communion without confession. . . . Cheap grace is grace without discipleship, and grace without the cross. . . ." We all want to feel better, but we don't want to change. We all want new life, but we don't want to suffer or die. The result, Bonhoeffer says, is that "we have watered the gospel down to an emotional uplift which makes no costly demands."[7]

If we dare to hear the gospel undiluted (or at least less diluted), what does it demand? Let's hear it one more time: "If any want to become my followers, let them deny themselves and take up their cross and follow me" (Matthew 16:24). Death is the door to new life. Jesus says, "Those who lose their life for my sake will find it" (Matthew 16:25). The key words, of course, are "for my sake." In and of itself, there is nothing holy or sacred about death or denial, and there is a big difference between being a doormat and being a disciple. The only reason we should deny ourselves, the only reason we should be willing to die, is for Jesus' sake. We let go of our baggage in order to follow him.

I read something very interesting from the philosopher Ken Wilber. He says religion has two functions, a horizontal one and a vertical one. The horizontal movement is to

---

7. Dietrich Bonhoeffer, *The Cost of Discipleship* (New York: Simon & Schuster, 1995), 45.

"create . . . meaning for the self " by offering myths and stories that help translate our experience into some coherent
pattern. But, he says, religion also has a vertical movement,
which is the movement of transformation. This function, he
says, "does not fortify the self but utterly shatters it. [It offers]
not consolation but devastation; . . . not complacency but
explosion."[8]

This is the vertical function of the cross: to put to death the
comfortable ways we think of ourselves and our world. The
cross shatters our self-image as well as our conception of others.
To see how it shatters our self-image, we must distinguish
between the false self and the true self.

The false self is who the world tells us we are: I am my accomplishments; I am my family; I am my possessions. While there is
nothing wrong with any of those, they are not at the center of
who we are, and they never give us a taste of eternal life.

Jesus says something else: he calls for us to remember our
true self as God's beloved child. God does not love us for what
we have done or what we possess or what we know. God loves
us because God is love. When we remember who we are, we
receive the grace to let go of all that keeps us trapped in the false
self. Jesus invites us to let go of our fear and live, and we are able
to do that only when we know in our gut that nothing—neither
failure, nor suffering, nor death itself—can separate us from the
love of Jesus Christ.

Still, most of us do not let go of our false self easily: it has
to be shattered. We have to bear the cross in order to embrace
our true self. Ask yourself what it is that needs to be shattered.
Is it your self-image? Your need to be right? Or perfect? Is it
your illusion that we have earned all that we have? Jesus says,
"If you want to follow me, all of that has to die." He doesn't
want the outside trappings of our false self; he wants us—he
wants our hearts.

---

8 . Ken Wilber, *One Taste: The Journals of Ken Wilber* (Boston: Shambhala, 1999),
27.

The shattering cross is seen in the disconsolate Peter just after he denies Jesus. It is seen in your spouse after he or she admits to being an alcoholic. It is seen in yourself when you have lost a job or a relationship: "If I am no longer who I thought I was, who am I now? Does God still love me? Do I still belong?" The cross is what brings us to our knees, but it is the doorway to love and life and Jesus Christ. We take up our cross and follow Jesus instead of our private little self. The life of the cross is not easy, and it is not comfortable, but it is real. That is why it's not cheap grace; it's costly grace. When it happens, you know in your bones that you belong to God.

> Amazing grace, how sweet the sound
> That saved a wretch like me.
> I once was lost, but now am found;
> Was blind, but now I see.

Beyond shattering our self-image, the cross shatters how we see others. It breaks through those categories we use to map the world, and we discover that we are members of one body, each of whom deserves to be treated with respect and love.

You can know someone who has never taken up the cross by the fact that he or she is certain about everything. He or she knows how the world works. The person understands all the theological issues of the day and knows who is a heretic and who is orthodox, but lacks compassion. In contrast, the women and men on the other side of the shattering know only the love of Jesus. They know that love is in everyone and what a waste of time it is to look for anything else. They know that it's all grace.

This summer I stayed with a family in Anthony, New Mexico. Marta, the mother, is in this country illegally, having walked across the border ten years ago. In Mexico, she was an accountant, but in Anthony, she cleans houses. Marta has four children, one of whom has a blood disorder that has stunted his growth so that he looks much younger than his age.

Now, I had come to New Mexico with certain ideas about the law and the rules. I had come to New Mexico with conceptions about the US economy and who needed American jobs. But when I looked at Marta's face as she watched her child, I simply saw every parent's face. I saw that strange mixture of joy and fear, hope and pain. I saw a parent who would do anything for her child. I didn't see the face of an illegal immigrant. Marta was me, or you, or the Madonna.

We live for each other and we die for each other because we share the common life of Jesus Christ. Sooner or later, Jesus shatters our categories, and we see him everywhere. And our lives are never the same.

No one wants to take up the cross. But if you want to live the Life, if you want to be in communion, if you want to follow Christ—the cross is the only Way.

DEMONS

He commands even the unclean spirits, and they obey him.

—Mark 1:27

Have you ever watched those faith healers on television? Be honest. When you saw them putting their hands on people's heads and screaming "Be healed!" didn't you feel sort of superior? Didn't you think to yourself, "Who could be so naïve or stupid as to believe in this stuff? It's only one step above professional wrestling."

There are parts of the Bible that are just a little embarrassing for us if we're honest. We really don't know what to do with them in this age of biological or physiological explanations. So it is with the story of exorcism from the Gospel of Mark. Jesus comes to the synagogue and astonishes the scribes with his teaching. So far, our comfort zone is intact. We like a smart Jesus just fine. But then things get a little strange. A man with an "unclean spirit" shows up and starts screaming and thrashing about, and Jesus rebukes the unclean spirit and orders it out. The crowd is "amazed."

32

What are we to do with this story? Should we just skip over it? If we don't skip it, are we placing Jesus alongside the television healers? Anglicans and other liberal Christians have always struggled with the question of demons and demonic possession. Because we like to stress grace so much, we often gloss over the reality of evil and the powers of darkness. We either make this passage so otherworldly that it has nothing to do with us or explain it away too easily. We say to ourselves, "The guy had epilepsy. It was psychosomatic, that's all."

We need to find a way into this story that makes it real for us. Clearly, Jesus was known as a healer and an exorcist, so if we toss out all the events that describe those behaviors, we will seriously reduce who Jesus is. What are we to do with this story?

Well, one thing we can say is that evil is a force that is real and that places people in bondage. Our images of evil are different from those in the Bible or even from our conservative Christian neighbors. We don't think of demons taking possession in quite the same way, but that doesn't mean that evil has been eradicated in our world. Unclean spirits—demons—the forces of darkness—are whatever binds us or enslaves us.

Jesus has come to bring people life—abundant life, the life that brings us closer to the people God created us to be. The word "salvation" means "wholeness." Jesus saves us from living a partial life and brings us closer to a whole life. The demon forces can be fear, or addiction, or prejudice or hatred or greed, or a whole long list of things that enslave us and cut us off from experiencing the love of God.

As I was thinking about this story, however, another way of reading it came to mind. I kept asking myself: When Jesus comes near the man with the unclean spirit, why does he thrash about? Why does the demon say, "What have you to do with us, Jesus of Nazareth? Have you come to destroy us?"

The demons not only know Jesus, they start to thrash around when he comes near. When they know that change is coming, they become disruptive. The man begins to shake because his life is about to be turned right side up.

There is a story from the Desert Fathers—third-century mystics who retreated to the desert to pray—that tells how a monk came to Abba Poeman and asked him, "Why do the demons fight against me?" The Abba answered, "The demons do not fight against us as long as we are doing our own will. When we seek to change, then our own wills become the demons, and it is these which attack us."

That turns the story inside out, doesn't it? The man who has the unclean spirit is the one on the road to transformation. God has started some work inside of him, and his life is thrashing about because he cannot accept the change. The release of Jesus, then, is not to "cure" the man but to help him change. Jesus is the one who removes what blocks the transformation God has started in us. Most of the time, we think that a cure for what ails us is to return to "normal," but we never go back to square one. Resurrection is always about new life. When Jesus comes out of the tomb, no one recognizes him at first. He looks like the gardener; he looks like a traveling companion; he looks like some guy on the beach . . . because he is not the same, and neither will we be after we, too, are transformed.

No wonder the man shakes! No wonder the people are astounded and amazed. The Greek word used here for "astounded" is *ekplessomai*, which means, literally, "blown out of their minds." Their minds aren't blown because the demon came out, but because Jesus is calling for them to be transformed as well. They know that sooner or later our calm, stable lives are going to start shaking. It isn't that they see the man as completely different from them. Instead, they know that today is his turn, but their turn is coming.

The Christian life is a journey: a journey to Bethlehem to be born, to Jerusalem to die, and to Emmaus to discover resurrection. Our God is dynamic, moving all of creation into wholeness. God is moving you and me and all people into being who we are created to be, and God is moving our societies into participating in the kingdom of peace and mercy and justice. That movement, that journey, blows our minds, because like the crowd, we know that we are next. The unclean spirit is the fear in us that wants to nail our lives down, that wants to nail down our Lord when he comes to bring us life. There is a demon in each of us that is afraid to hit the road, and that fear is what makes us shake.

The good news is that shaking is the first sign of life, but the best news is that the love who is Jesus Christ is greater than our fear! "Have you come to destroy us?" the unclean spirits ask. The answer is, "Yes, but that's not all. I have come to give you life."

Jesus is not a magician, and he is not a therapist. He doesn't make us feel good, and he doesn't make us change against our will. He certainly doesn't help us cope with this world and keep pretending that all is well. Jesus is the one who brings us life, the one who battles the powers of death and darkness within us and pulls us, shaking and screaming, into resurrection.

In the film *Magnolia*, the character of Frank "T. J." Mackie is a new kind of self-help guru, peddling his own program to teach men how to seduce women. He is smooth and polished, and he has an answer and a technique for every problem or condition. He tells a news reporter that the past is the past; it's a waste of time to look behind. But try as he might, Frank has to look behind. He is forced to reunite with his dying father. When Frank goes to see him, he kneels beside the bed and begins to curse his father for having abandoned him as a boy. This is the past that Frank would like to leave behind, but it is also the demon that has cut him off from life, the demon that has pushed him to adopt such a twisted perspective on life. He kneels before his father and says, "I am not going to cry for you," but he starts to shake, first in his shoulders and then in his whole body. He shakes and shakes, and the tears roll down his face. As he shakes, it is as if Jesus is there, saying, "Be silent and come out of him." Frank grabs his father's hand and finds peace. It's his turn.

So, the question to us is not whether we believe in unclean spirits or demons or exorcisms. The question is, is our quietness and calmness *real* calm, or are we like Frank, covering over whatever blocks us from abundant life? And if we are like

Frank, are we prepared to realize that when we shake and trem-
ble, it is a sign of Jesus bringing us new life?

DISCIPLINE

For the Lord disciplines those whom he loves.

—Hebrews 12:6

In 1977 I received my first promotion: from being a teacher of
tenth- and twelfth-grade English to being the assistant principal of the private high school where I had been teaching. I was
delighted to get an office and a secretary, not to mention a
raise. It was only after the glow of all these perks began to dim
that I realized what my primary duty was: student discipline.

I confess, I was not very good at it. Actually, I was terrible at
it. I am sure there are many reasons why I did not flourish in
this position—such as my temperament or my being only
twenty-seven—but the chief reason is that I never had any real
vision of the job.

The students at this school had to wear uniforms, which
meant that the teachers would send Billy down to Mr. Taylor's
office because he didn't have socks the right color or because he
was wearing tennis shoes or sandals, or they'd send Susie
because her blouse wasn't the right shade of blue or her skirt
was too short. I would have to punish them, because that's
what the book said I had to do, but my heart wasn't in it. I
couldn't figure out what difference it made whether Billy's
socks were blue or red. I didn't think the world would end if
every last student wore red ones, and I didn't think "the kingdom" would come if everyone's uniforms were picture-perfect.

I did care passionately about some behaviors, like whether
the students went to class or treated their teachers with respect,
but not uniforms or parking permits or noise in the lunch-
room. After two years, I resigned, because for me *discipline* had

become the same as *punishment*. I wasn't interested in being
the chief of police for a high school; I was interested in helping
students learn and grow.

I think my confusion about the difference between discipline and punishment is pretty common. Perhaps that confusion is why this passage from the Letter to the Hebrews sounds
so harsh to our ears. "The Lord disciplines those whom he loves"
sounds like our parents saying, "I'm doing this because I love
you," right before they ground us for a month.

However, "discipline" has another meaning. The Greek word
is *paideia*, and it means "to learn" or "to apprentice," or even "to
get to know." *Paideia* means to learn a way of life or a skill by
entering into relationship with a master. The apprentice imitates
the master. That's why "discipline" has the same root as "disciple."

But if you have the wrong master, discipline always feels like
punishment. There was no way I was ever going to be a good
assistant principal, even if I found the toughest assistant principal around and imitated everything he or she did, because being
an assistant principal wasn't in my nature. I had no vision of
why I should work to get better at it. When we are learning what
is false to who we are, there is no joy in discipline.

In contrast, the kind of discipline that the Letter to the
Hebrews is describing is a joyful enterprise. The *paideia*, or
learning, is joyful because it connects us to who we are. As we
discipline ourselves, what is false falls away, and our true nature
flourishes. Of course, this discipline is hard because ridding
ourselves of what is false is never easy. We are constantly losing
our way and getting stuck in destructive patterns of behavior.
Shedding the weight of sin, turning around from the dark to
the light, turns out to be harder than we might have expected,
but in our hearts and souls we know it is right. We know that
it brings us life.

So, how are we to discipline ourselves? I think learning—
true change—comes when we have a glimpse of the truth, and
that glimpse makes us want to see more, makes us willing to
discipline ourselves. One day we meet someone who is doing

the very thing we have always secretly longed to do, and the vision of that person compels us to learn to play the piano or practice law or become a scientist. One day we see a painting and say, "I'd give my life to paint like that." One day we *look out* but we *see in*, and a voice inside us says, "That is what I am born for."

That vision is what motivates us to go through the hard work of learning. Without the vision, it's just punishment, but with the vision, it is an unfolding affirmation of who we are. Whatever our talent is—writing, cooking, gardening, playing tennis—isn't cultivated without work, but the work often doesn't feel like work because we have a vision of who we are meant to be and are becoming.

The Letter to the Hebrews helps us understand discipline with regard to all of our activities and professions, but it is ultimately about a deeper calling: our calling to grow into the likeness of Christ, which is the destiny of every Christian. Remember how the passage begins?

"Therefore, since we are surrounded by so great a cloud of witnesses, let us also lay aside every weight and the sin that clings so closely, and let us run with perseverance the race that is set before us, looking to Jesus the pioneer and perfecter of our faith" (Hebrews 12:1–2).

Since we are surrounded by examples of women and men who have led holy lives, since we look to Jesus as the prime example, since we have a vision of our destiny as lovers of God, we can lay aside the weight that slows us down and run the race. We are drawn by the vision to change, to discipline our lives to move toward the goal.

I learned what it meant to be a Christian by encountering authentic people of faith and wanting to be like them. I met people like Arthur Evans, a professor of comparative literature at Emory University. He showed me what it meant to be faithful: he could be calm in a chaotic world because he knew that Jesus Christ loved him. Arthur had Parkinson's disease, and it wracked his body. He could speak five languages, but as the disease progressed, he would lose the ability to speak at all. One day when I was with him, I cried out in frustration, "Why you, Dr. Evans? Why you?" He said, "Why not me? I have had a wonderful life."

On that day, I knew that I wanted to be like him. That vision of faithfulness helps me discipline myself to grow, to quiet my petty voices when they want to complain about my minor tribulations. The surprise of my life has been to discover that now, on my best days, I am an example for others. And so are you, because that's the way it works: I get the vision from you; you get the vision from me. We receive it and pass it along.

The cloud of witnesses includes both the saints who have gone before and the saints here today. We are to show one another what it means to love the Lord; what it means to act for justice; what it means to sacrifice ourselves for another person. We are to show one another what it means to lead moral lives, to practice forgiveness, to be people of prayer.

The early church was sometimes called "the School of Love." Sometimes we are the teachers, and sometimes we are the students, but we help one another discipline ourselves to grow into the likeness of Christ. We remind one another of our common destiny to be saints—to be Christlike. The School of Love is that great cloud of witnesses, the saints around us that help us catch the vision and discipline our lives. These saints are everywhere, as the hymn says:

> One was a doctor and one was a queen
> And one was a shepherdess on the green
> All of them saints of God
> And I mean, God helping, to be one too.

EQUIPMENT

"Take no gold, or silver, or copper in your belts, no bag
for your journey, or two tunics, or sandals, or a staff."

—Matthew 10:9–10

Every time we baptize someone into the body of Christ, we
renew our own baptismal covenant. We renew all those promises
that we made or someone made for us in our baptism. Do you
remember them? Do you remember how impossible they are? To
seek and serve Christ in all people, to strive for justice and peace
among all people, to respect the dignity of all persons, to perse-
vere in resisting evil, and to proclaim by word and example the
Good News of God in Christ.

How is a child supposed to do those things? More to the
point, how are we? We are all too busy, and none of us has any
training in this stuff. We don't have time to go to the bookstore
and buy some manual called *Twelve Steps to Being an Effective
Disciple of Jesus Christ*.

However, let us keep hope, because the work doesn't depend
on us. Doing God's work is not about our becoming accomplished

in special skills. There are no tryouts; the question is not "How can I do God's work in the world?" but "How can I participate in what God is already doing?"

When Jesus gives the twelve disciples their marching orders, their tasks are even harder than ours: cure the sick, raise the dead, cleanse the lepers. No doubt the disciples were wide-eyed when they heard this. "*Us*? You want *us* to do *that*?"

In fact, Jesus tells them how to do it, but we might not have heard the secret formula because the words are so familiar. Here is a different translation that takes some liberties: "Don't begin by traveling to some far-off place to convert unbelievers, and don't try to be dramatic by tackling some public enemy. Go to the lost, confused people right here in the neighborhood. Tell them the kingdom is here. Don't think you have to hold a fund-raising campaign before you start, either. You don't need a lot of equipment. You *are* the equipment."[1]

We hear that and say to ourselves, "Maybe Jesus doesn't know how complicated the world is." When we think of our world and its problems, we can't believe that these instructions are adequate. To heal the injustice in the world, we need to form a committee or get a consultant and set goals and objectives and get tax-deductible status. And stationery! Who knows? Maybe we'll get on the *Oprah Winfrey Show* or at least get some award for being wonderful people.

So long as we make doing Christ's work a grandiose enterprise, we delude ourselves about the real task at hand and keep our egos at the center. But Jesus says we don't need a lot of tools for our work because we *are* the tools for God's work. God is already at work redeeming the world. All we need to do is put ourselves in the way of what God is doing.

When we do, we find that Jesus is calling us to the way of freedom and grace. Rather than fixating on having the right tools and technique, rather than letting our egos keep control,

---

1. Eugene H. Peterson, *The Message* (Colorado Springs: NAVPress, 1995), 31.

we are being asked to make a radical realignment. Jesus is calling for us to walk in the Way of the Lord and see what happens.

Six hundred years ago, a wealthy Italian teenager was confused about what to do with his life. His father wanted him to go into the family business, but that didn't quite fit who he was. He wanted to help people, but he didn't know how. After all, he had no special gifts or advanced theological degrees. Finally, he went over to the church and opened the Bible and randomly put his finger down on the page. When he looked down, his finger pointed to this very passage: "Take no equipment. You are the equipment." And when he read Jesus' instructions, the way of freedom and grace opened before him. His name was Francisco di Pietro di Bernardone, but he is better known as St. Francis of Assisi.

Francis formed no committee or task force. He didn't read any books and he didn't go to get trained. He didn't go to Asia or Africa to perform heroic deeds. He just became part of God's work in his own hometown. He knew that God was calling him to be a healing presence in a hurting world.

Now, I know that we think of St. Francis as being way above us in terms of being spiritual. He is a saint, after all. But that is just a way of getting ourselves off the hook. In Baptism, we are given as much equipment as Francis had, for we are promised that we are Christ's own forever. Wherever we go, Christ will be there.

I think Woody Allen had it right when he said that 90 percent of success is just showing up. Ninety percent of fulfilling all those promises we make in our baptismal covenant comes from our showing up and letting God work through us. Unfortunately, though, most of us are no-shows. We are too worried about how to do it right or about what will happen to us if we take that risk.

When I was a seminarian, I spent a summer as a chaplain in a hospital in Chattanooga, Tennessee, and part of my assignment was the intensive care unit. One of the patients I visited was a woman who was unconscious most of the time and could not talk even when she was conscious. I went to see her every day, but I was always nervous and anxious. I didn't know what to say or what to do; none of the books I had read covered this. I had some wonderful theological answers for why we suffer, but she didn't seem very interested. Finally, one day I gave up trying to figure out the right tactic and just sat down and held her hand. Finally, I got out of the way so that God could bring us into a holy communion. I showed up. And suddenly I realized that ministry is *not about me*. Ministry is about God in Christ through the Holy Spirit saving the world.

Once we know that, we are free to participate in that divine activity. So, I have some strange instructions for you. Stop trying to get it right. Stop trying to be a hero. Put all those self-help books back on the shelf. Forget drawing up a five-year plan that will solve all the world's problems. We don't need another savior—we already have one.

Send your fears into the corner and start doing the work God has given you to do, right where you are. Don't wait until you can go to Haiti; start on your way home today. Don't form a committee; look into the eyes of the next person you meet. Believe that God has sent you where you are and that God has equipped you to bring the Good News of Jesus Christ to the people surrounding you. If you still don't know where to start, let me make a suggestion.

TIME magazine once quoted Mother Teresa as saying that loneliness was the leprosy of our time. That's right, loneliness—not cancer, not AIDS. So, if you're overwhelmed by all those baptismal promises about peace and justice and serving Christ in all persons, begin with loneliness. We are called to be free as Francis was free: to look into the face of whoever comes along and greet that person as our brother or sister. For Francis, there wasn't a good side or a bad side of town. There weren't any acceptable or unacceptable people; there weren't any divisions between race or class. Francis looked all the way into the person in front of him, then took his or her hands and let God do the rest.

Once a man stood before God, his heart breaking from the pain and injustice in the world. "Dear God," he cried out, "Look at all the suffering, the anguish and distress in your world. Why don't you send help?" God responded, "I did send help. I sent you."[2]

EVANGELISM

"Do you understand what you are reading?" He replied, "How can I, unless someone guides me?"

—Acts 8:30–31

During the Great Fifty Days of Easter, the days between Easter Sunday and Pentecost, the Church reads from the Book of the Acts of the Apostles and remembers the story of how the Church was born. We read how this small group of people wrestled with what to do in the face of the incredible news of the resurrection of their Lord. The Acts of the Apostles gives us a map for how the faith spreads and how that growth shapes and changes the movement they called "the Way" and we call "the Church."

We can learn a lot from the Acts of the Apostles, because there is something about spreading the faith that makes us nervous. Just the word "evangelism" makes us squirm. We think of people coming to our door telling us what they think is wrong with our current beliefs and why we have to believe exactly what they believe. Evangelism makes us think of someone trying to take us hostage. Reversing roles doesn't help, either. Our lives are so pluralistic that we aren't always sure how to spread the faith and still respect other people's distinctiveness.

---

2. David Wolfe, *Teaching Your Children about God* (New York: Holt, 1993). Quoted in *Spiritual Literacy: Reading the Sacred in Everyday Life*, ed. Frederic and Mary Ann Brussat (New York: Scribner, 1996), 327.

Our world is alphabet soup, and many of the letters aren't even in our alphabet.

So, how are we to take seriously the promise we make at baptism "to spread by word and example the Good News of God in Christ"? How can we be evangelists in a pluralistic world? The scripture passage about Philip and the Ethiopian helps by highlighting three components essential to the sharing of faith: there is a beginning and middle and ending.

In the beginning of Acts, the writer tells us that the Spirit moves Philip to go down a *wilderness* road and to approach the Ethiopian. The writer emphasizes that these characters are in wilderness and in transit. The Spirit moves us out from our comfortable places into the messy, changing world in which we live. We have to move out to encounter people in the wilderness of actual life. Sometimes we in the Church are so caught up in our own little church world that we forget that most of the people who are uninvolved have no idea why any of it matters. I have never met any unchurched person who wanted to know about transubstantiation. However, many people want to know if there is any meaning in their journey. They want to hear what the Church has to say to their deepest concerns: "What can you tell me about suffering? Does your faith have anything to do with my life?"

The middle of the story is an encounter, a place of meeting. The Ethiopian invites Philip to come into his chariot and explain the scriptures. Without this invitation, it doesn't matter how important Philip thinks his message is. Our job is to be where people are as they journey along their way, but we can't force the message onto people who don't want to hear. All we can do is wait for the invitation, then respond with an invitation of our own: an invitation into the body of Christ, an invitation to love.

My mother lives on the South Carolina coast. Years ago when I would drive to visit her, I would see a billboard on a state highway that read LOVE JESUS OR ROT IN HELL. Somehow that doesn't sound like an invitation. Really, it's kind of laughable.

How can you possibly command love? Sharing our faith means that we are responding to what God is already doing. We become aware of the Spirit moving in us and in other people. God opens people's hearts, and we must listen for their invitation. As we listen, we must pay attention to what they are asking and what they are not. The Ethiopian wants to know the reference for the passage in Isaiah; he doesn't want to know who is going to hell and who isn't. The Ethiopian wants to hear that through Jesus Christ we discover that God loves us more than we ever could imagine. The Good News is that God is incarnated in our lives; the Word has become flesh all around us. If anyone is going to receive that news, it is only going to be as an answer to what is asked.

Finally, the end of the story isn't really an ending. We know that the Ethiopian has changed and that his whole orientation is different. The meaningless words suddenly point their way to a new Savior, and instead of being only the treasurer for the queen, he is now a Christian. Evangelism is not like delivering a package and then going on with one's life. Evangelism is about relationship; therefore, it changes everyone and everything. Because it is an encounter, the messenger is also changed.

The little band of Jesus' followers didn't have many rules. Philip is not sure exactly how this church thing is going to work. The Ethiopian says to him, "What is to prevent me from being baptized?" In other words, "Can your Jesus movement incorporate the new?" The Ethiopian doesn't ask whether this has ever been done before. He asks, "Why not?" Philip learns that because the faith is alive, the shape of the Church—the ways we put the faith into play—is always changing. Philip leaves the encounter with a new idea of what this Jesus movement is all about. "What is to prevent me from being baptized?" What is to prevent the Church from opening up to Gentiles, to different races? What is to prevent the Church from accepting African Americans in the 1960s? Or ordaining women in the 1970s? Is it the Good News that says no to these questions or just our stubbornness? Is it God's will or just our inability to move with the Spirit onto the wilderness road, where the new waits to meet us? I am always amazed at how much time we spend tearing other people down instead of proclaiming grace. You cannot build on negativity. You have to know what you are for and what you base your life on. You cannot define an identity simply by pointing to what you are not.

In the early 1960s, a Benedictine monk named Bede Griffiths went to Madras, India, to build a monastery. Because he was a proper Benedictine, he built the monastery along traditional lines: a large, square building with an interior walkway. After some time there, he was called by the Spirit onto the wilderness road that led into the city, and he discovered that although he and his brothers had taken vows of poverty, they lived in the nicest building around. He also discovered that the Benedictines didn't have a monopoly on prayer and the spiritual life: the Indians knew something about these things, too.

So he asked himself, "What is to prevent me from responding creatively to where I am?" The monks gave away their newly built monastery and built huts of straw like everyone else. Bede Griffiths got permission from the Pope to change his traditional Benedictine dress for orange robes like Hindu monks wear. He began to invite the local people to Mass and to incorporate their Hindu chants into the liturgy. Christianity became alive in Madras because Bede Griffiths responded to the people that invited him to share the Good News with them.

This story of Philip and the Ethiopian is the first story of the Church's reaching beyond its Jewish origins to accept someone different, but the story never ends. We are always called by the Spirit out of our safe boxes and onto the wilderness road. Once there, we are to look for invitations into other people's lives and to share the Good News they long to hear. We are to recognize that God is changing us as God changes the hearts of those we encounter. Spreading the Good News is not a marketing plan for the Church; it's God's way of calling the Church to stay alive.

FALL

She took of its fruit and ate; and she also gave some to her husband, who was with her, and he ate. Then the eyes of both were opened.

—Genesis 3:6–7

Richard Rohr, the Franciscan writer, says every very healthy religion has to give its people three kinds of stories: creation stories that tell us where we came from, pattern stories that give a sense of how our existence is meaningful, and end stories that tell us where we are going. If we are to be whole and centered, we have to have these three kinds of stories.

In this reading from Genesis, we hear part of our creation story: Adam and Eve and the fall from the garden. Yet, what do we really hear? Sometimes stories get used up. They are so familiar to us that we can no longer hear anything new in them. Because we think we know exactly what they mean, we hear only our own interpretations of them. Perhaps that is what you hear in this story: that the snake is evil, or that the fall is all Eve's fault, or that God is eternally angry and humans are worthless sinners. Instead, let's look at the story again and see if we can hear it in a fresh way.

First of all, what is Eden? Eden is the land before time, a place without death, a place of eternal summer. Eden is other-worldly because it is static: nothing happens in Eden. The first humans are one with the world around them and know the true names of all things, but the first humans have no wills. They do not create anything; they only appreciate what already is. They are not active agents in the world.

We call the first humans Adam and Eve, but in the Hebrew these are not really proper names. "Adam" means "human"—literally, "earth creature"—and "Eve" means "life." In Eden, Adam and Eve lack personality or even identities, because in this place before time people are unconscious of themselves. They have no sense of self.

This brings us to the infamous tree: the tree of knowledge, the tree of good and evil, the tree of consciousness. As soon as Adam and Eve eat the fruit, their eyes are opened and they know that they are naked. This is the beginning of the fashion business: they start to have an image of themselves, and immediately they worry about how they look.

The more profound result, however, is that suddenly the world isn't just a place to admire. Suddenly, Adam and Eve become actors in a drama—and they know it. This is frightening. Their lives instantly become more complicated and more fragile, and they don't know whether things will work out. *What if our sons kill one another? What if our grandchildren are threatened by a flood? What if our descendants are exiled as slaves in a far-away place?*

The world of time is a world of possibilities and risks. It is the world of "What if?" Once Adam and Eve's eyes are opened, they have to leave the garden of no time, and the world begins. God tells them, "I have good news and bad news. The good news is that you are now creators. You are now empowered by your imagination and wills to be fruitful. You can give birth to children and crops and cities and civilizations. The bad news is that all fruition has a cost. Eve, you will labor in childbirth. Adam, you will labor in the fields." The next thing God does is to clothe them for their new life.

I like to imagine one other scene in the story, which I think is true even if it's reading between the lines. Just as Adam and Eve are walking out the gates of the garden, into this new world, God sees that they are very excited but very frightened, and so God says to them, "I will always be with you. And one day—one day, we'll walk in a garden together again."

This is our story. We are people who had to fall to be who we are. Why else would God have put the tree there in the first place? God knew that humans would eat the fruit—they *had* to. The reason God told them not to eat from that tree is the same reason we tell ten-year-olds not to watch R-rated movies, the same reason parents cry when their baby starts first grade: we want to keep children innocent as long as we can, because once you eat the fruit, you are on your own. You can never go back to the timeless garden. As the poet Dylan Thomas wrote, "After the first death, there is no other" ("A Refusal to Mourn the Death, by Fire, of a Child in London").

Our primal story tells us that we came from God, that life is always birth and pain, and that living in time is both a glorious and scary enterprise. We can bring the story full circle by placing it next to another story that happens at the other end of the Bible. In the Gospel of John, a long time later, we find ourselves in another garden: Joseph of Arimathea and Nicodemus are in a garden, where they lay the body of Jesus in a tomb. After three days, Mary Magdalene comes to this place early in the morning, and she sees someone walking there.

Mary is not Eve, and this is not Eden. Most of the disciples have chosen not to be here and are in hiding. Mary knows that she is in a world where amazing things can happen: people like herself—people with seven demons inside them—can be healed, and people can also crucify the one who healed her. It's the world of birth and pain, the world of time.

Mary sees someone in walking in the garden, and do you know who she thought the someone was? She thought it was the gardener. At least, she thought this until he said her name. Then she said his, and once more heaven and earth were joined—but this time, this time the human creature was aware. And maybe for that awareness, that moment, the fall from Eden was worth it.

FORGIVENESS

> Then Peter came and said to him, "Lord, if another member of the church sins against me, how often should I forgive?"
>
> —Matthew 18:21

Peter asks Jesus, "How often should I forgive? As many as seven times?" To his astonishment, Jesus said to him, "Not seven times, but, I tell you, seventy-seven times." We know what Peter said under his breath, or at least we know what we would have said, "*Get real*. I was stretching to offer seven. In fact, I was stretching to offer to forgive at all, and you say seventy-seven? No way."

Forgiveness is hard—it is an unnatural act. When someone wrongs us, our reaction is either fight or flight. We either step back from the person and lick our wounds in private, or we want to get even. We think, "You hurt me—I'll hurt you. And eye for an eye; a tooth for a tooth."

Oh, we can always fake it. Someone criticizes us or ignores us or hurts us, and we say, "Forget it. It doesn't matter. It's no big deal." But it is. We hurt and in that hurt, we aren't focused on forgiveness; we are focused on justice. We don't want to say, "I forgive you"; we want to say, "I want you to know how much I hurt and I hope you hurt some too." Forgive seventy-seven times? You have got to be kidding.

Forgiveness is hard, but it is possible and it is an essential part of our calling as Christians. So what is forgiveness? Well, let's remember what it is not. Forgiveness is not being a doormat or a punching bag. Nor is forgiveness swallowing our anger and pretending everything is wonderful. We are not to put on a happy face while we are boiling underneath. We always have to work through our feelings and not around them. Forgiveness only comes after our anger evaporates.

Forgiveness is also not the same as reconciliation. Reconciliation requires that both parties change and meet again. But we cannot control what anyone else does. We cannot make the other person become reconciled to us. Sometimes the person we need to forgive is physically separate or even dead.

If forgiveness is not the same as denial or reconciliation, what is it?

Forgiveness is about *our* conversion. That's right, our conversion, and not the conversion of the person who wronged us. To forgive another person who has caused us harm, we have to change the way we see them. There's a cartoon showing two restrooms. Instead of MEN and WOMEN, they said VICTIM and OPPRESSOR.[1] When we have been wronged, when we have been hurt, we see the other person only in terms of what they have done to us. We say to ourselves: *You are the person who has hurt me. That is who you are. I do not want to know any more about you. I am not interested in even knowing why. I just want you out of my life and I want you to suffer more than I have.*

The refusal to forgive harms us, not the other person. Remember *The Scarlet Letter*? Arthur Dimmesdale has committed adultery with Hester Prynne. After some years, Hester's husband, Roger Chillingworth, returns home to find his wife with a child not his. As Roger discerns that Dimmesdale is the father, he systematically exacts his revenge.

---

1. Richard Rohr, *Hope Against Darkness* (Cincinnati, OH: St. Anthony Messenger Press, 2001), 85.

Chillingworth psychologically torments his foe—because he cannot forgive him. Chillingworth becomes locked in a cycle of retribution.

However, the important point is that Dimmesdale is able to experience a conversion at the novel's end. Dimmesdale is able to confess his sin and find peace, but Chillingworth cannot. As a result, he becomes demonic. Because he cannot and will not see Dimmesdale as a whole person, he cannot be a whole person.

When Dimmesdale dies, Hawthorne writes that Chillingworth "withered up, shriveled away . . . like an uprooted weed that lies wilting in the sun."[2] He has no identity outside his sense of being victimized. If we cannot forgive, then our lives become stuck. We cannot grow; we cannot flourish. The worst sinner in the novel is not either of the two people committing adultery; the worst sinner is that man who cannot forgive.

Forgiveness is accepting a whole vision of the other person. When we forgive someone else, we see the person as God sees him or her and as God sees us. We realize that we are all sinners; we are all flawed people capable of hurting one another. We have all "erred and strayed like lost sheep," but we are also children of God; we also belong to Jesus Christ. When we forgive someone, we don't discount what they have done, but we know that they are more than their sin against us. We pray for them; we long for them to come home and be the person God created them to be. Roger Chillingworth should have desired that Dimmesdale do the hard work of confession and penance to reach the new life of absolution. Instead, he tries to keep him from telling anyone because he doesn't want to let go of his self-righteous anger.

The Dalai Lama tells a story about a Tibetan monk who had served eighteen years in a Chinese prison in Tibet. The monk came to see the Dalai Lama. During their meeting the Dalai

---

2. Nathaniel Hawthorne, *The Scarlet Letter* (New York: Norton, 1988), 175.

Lama asked the monk what he felt was the biggest danger while
he was in captivity. The monk said what he feared most was
losing his compassion for the Chinese.

Forgiveness is hard because it demands us to be willing to
meet the other person if he or she will come to the table. To
forgive, we have to give up our own self-righteousness. We have
to stop dividing the world between victims and oppressors.

There's a story from the desert tradition of the third century.
A brother had committed a wrong and a council was called to
judge him. The abba was invited to come, but he refused to go.
The brothers sent someone to fetch him. After much pleading,
he got up and went. He took a jug with him that had a leak in
it. He filled it with water and put it under his arm. The other
monks came out to greet him and said, "What is this, Father?"

The old man answered. "My sins run out behind me and I
do not see them, and today I am coming to judge the errors of
another." When the brothers heard this, they went in and forgave the brother at fault.[3]

There are not two doors labeled "victims" and "oppressors."
There are two places: heaven and hell. Heaven is filled with forgiven sinners who recognize their own limits and know that
only God in Christ has rescued them from the death of sinfulness or self-righteousness. Forgiven sinners know that all of life
is an endless exchange of sin and forgiveness.

Hell is also filled with forgiven sinners, except that these
people cannot accept forgiveness nor can they give it. Hell is
filled with people who know they have been wronged and are
waiting for God to look at their scorecard and make things right.

We can insist on separating the world into the righteous
and the evildoers if we choose to do so. More than likely we will
live in hell waiting for God to punish the evil ones. Instead,
Jesus asks that we remember how often God has forgiven our
trespasses. Jesus asks that we work through our anger and hurt

---

3. *The Desert Christian: Sayings of the Desert Fathers*, trans. Benedicta Ward (New
York: Macmillan, 1975), 139.

and self-righteousness so that we can look at the person who has harmed us and realize that, just like us, that person isn't a evildoer but is a forgiven child of God.

FREEDOM

> You were called to freedom . . . but through love become slaves to one another.
>
> —Galatians 5:13

The summer before my freshman year at the University of North Carolina was a time of great excitement. Finally, after eighteen years of living under my parents' roof, I was going to be free. I could party all night and sleep all day. No more vegetables, no more cleaning my room, no more "looking nice" . . . the four years stretched out in front of me like an oasis of undiluted self-indulgence.

And in fact, some of my expectations were fulfilled. The only vegetable I ate in the city limits of Chapel Hill during my freshman year was the pickles on hamburgers. It is also true that my wardrobe was limited to T-shirts and jeans, and sometimes I did party all night and sleep all day. But I quickly discovered that college was not the lawless world I had envisioned. As it turned out, my professors did not recognize my right to undiluted self-indulgence. They actually had expectations of me. They wanted me to read books and write papers and come to science labs and memorize vocabulary. After the first week of college, my dream of freedom was shattered. Yes, I could choose when and how to do the work, but doing the work meant saying goodbye to freedom. I had swapped my parents' list of expectations for a list of assignments four years long.

Only one thing saved me: I went to my literature class and walked into a new world. I confess that math and science and foreign languages were always work for me—studying them was like having to clean my room. But not literature or history or religion. These courses were invitations to see the world through a different lens, and the more I saw, the more I wanted to see. However, in order to see more, I had to learn the rules and discipline my vision.

I found that college—like anything worth doing—had its own set of rules. Yes, I was free from my parents, but if I wanted to belong, I was not completely free. The good news was that I willingly gave up my freedom: the joy of discovering the beauty of John Donne was worth the pain of the rules.

So, during my four years of college, sometimes I did stay up all night partying, but sometimes I also stayed up all night reading. If college had been only work, I would not have made it. We do not willingly give up our freedom for another form of duty. No, the only catalyst that enables us to serve a discipline is love. We give up our freedom for love.

I use the example of my college days because we have a hard time with the concept of freedom. Too often, we think of freedom as license to do whatever we want. We think in terms of the individual asserting his or her rights. Freedom is freedom from obligations and duties and expectations. Party all night; sleep all day.

However, that is not the Christian notion of freedom. That's not St. Paul's message to the Galatians. The Christians in Galatia were Gentiles who converted to Christianity. Just when they thought they were free, some Jewish Christians threaten them with having to follow all of the Mosaic laws. Before Paul's letter, the Galatians felt as if they have finally gotten out of high school only to discover four years of assignments ahead of them.

Paul tells the new Gentile Christians—and the Jewish Christians—that Christian freedom is different from what either of them thought. It's not a life of license to do whatever you want, but it also isn't a life of rules. Like so much in Christianity, freedom is a paradox: "For freedom Christ has set us free. . . . Do not submit again to a yoke of slavery. . . . but through love become slaves of one another" (Galatians 5:1, 13).

Christ sets us free—but to become servants in a different way. What must the Galatians have made of this? Indeed, what are we who live in the land of the free to make of it?

Martin Luther once wrote that there are two essential truths to being a Christian: "A Christian is a free lord of all, subject to none. A Christian is a dutiful servant of all, subject to all." This is the great paradox of the Christian life. We are no longer bound by the law, but we are bound by the love of Jesus, and that love binds us to one another.

Grace, the gift that cannot be earned, has set us free from being slaves to the law. Because we have felt God's love—that amazing grace—we are free from the world's silly games. We can step outside the ways of the world that say our worth is measured in power and possessions and prestige. We are free because we know who we are—children of God. Freedom for us is not about creating yourself in your own image, but about finding the Creator's love for you in your own soul.

We are set free from the anxiety of the world to love one another as Christ loves us, which means that the love that sets us free binds us to our brothers and sisters. Therefore, the sign of our freedom is finally the sign of the cross. Because Jesus was free, he was not afraid of what the world could do to him. He would not bow down to Pilate or play the political game. He would not cut a deal so that someone else would suffer and he would keep his resume intact. He was free to love without fear and to live and die for us.

Once we know Christ's love for us, everything changes. That love changes how we see and act toward other people. I didn't study John Donne because I had to; I studied his poetry because I fell in love with it. In like manner, once we know God loves us, we see every person in a new light of love, because Jesus Christ is in them, too.

There is a story about a guest master at a Benedictine monastery whose job is to greet the people who come on retreat, strangers from all walks of life. He said that he sees them coming up the walk toward the monastery—all shapes,

all sizes, different races, different backgrounds—yet sometimes, when the light is a certain way, he catches his breath
and squints his eyes and says to himself, "Oh, Jesus Christ. Is
it you again?"[4]

We are to serve one another not because we have to, not
because we are trying to win God's affection by doing the right
thing, but because the nature of love is to love.

FRIENDS

"I do not call you servants any longer . . . but I have called
you friends."

—John 15:15

It's ten o'clock at night and I'm packing to leave tomorrow for
the annual diocesan convention. I'm looking for socks that
match and wondering where in the world my hanging bag is
and trying to figure out what we can possibly talk about for two
days at this convention. So when the phone rings, I pick it up
with less than enthusiasm.

"It's Frank. My mom died. Can you come?"

Suddenly I am back in Asheville, North Carolina, in 1964.
There is a new kid in our neighborhood. He's from Yonkers,
New York, and he talks funny and he wears weird shoes. But he
plays basketball, and I like him. We become friends.

Frank and I like hanging out together. We laugh at the same
jokes and listen to the same music. We talk about which girls to
ask out, about what to do when they say no, or—even scarier—
what to do when they say yes. Frank and I stay friends through
high school and go to college together. The night he calls, we
have been friends for thirty-three years. There is only one
answer to his question, "Can you come?" It is, "I'll be there."

---

4. Kathleen Norris, *Dakota* (New York: Ticknor & Fields, 1993), 191.

Jesus says, "I do not call you servants any longer . . . but I have called you friends." *Friends*—not slaves, not workers, not children, but *friends*. What does being friends with Jesus imply?

First, friends are loyal. They are connected to one another. We think of the Three Musketeers: "All for one, and one for all!" It's true. Friends stand up for you. Whenever I feel blue, whenever my ego is in sore need of repair, I call one of my friends. I don't usually ask for advice; just talking to her makes me feel better, because I know my friend loves me just for me. I think that's why Frank called me to come: not to say anything special, but to be there for him.

In the film *The Natural*, Roy Hobbs is a baseball player who comes up for his last at-bat after he has struck out all day long. As he stands behind the plate, the woman who loves him stands up in the middle of the seated crowd. That's my image of friendship. Jesus calls us friends because he wants us to know that he will be there for us, and he expects us to be there for him.

Second, friendship is not exclusive, like romantic love is. In its purest form, friendship is inclusive. I know that kids have all sorts of conversations about "best friends," but that isn't friendship in its purest form. Friendship delights in expansion. Friends are not threatened when someone else is included. Frank came from Yonkers, yet he became part of a circle of friends. I didn't have to choose between being friends with him or with someone else.

The word "companion" literally means "together at bread." Our image of friends should be all of us together at the table with our Lord. The closer we are to him, the closer we are to each other, and vice versa. Jesus tells us we are his friends because he wants us to grow in love: in our love for him, in our love for one another, and in our love for those we don't yet know.

Finally, friendship is joyous. C. S. Lewis says, "Friendship is unnecessary, like philosophy, like art, like the universe itself (for God did not need to create). It has no survival value; rather it

is one of those things which give value to survival."[5] You can eat
by yourself in a restaurant, but who wants to? Friends are part
of what gives our world color. I like my friends because we
make each other laugh; they bring out parts of me that would
remain hidden otherwise. We can relax with friends—they
know us and we know them, so we can be who we truly are
with each other.

At his mother's funeral, I didn't care whether Frank was
appropriately sad or religious or if he said the right things. We
just took a walk, and he talked about his Mom and his Dad and
what a roller coaster he'd been on. We talked about who was
there and who wasn't, and whatever happened to so-and-so,
and even about his dog back in 1964. "I have called you
friends," Jesus says, "because I want you to enjoy this gift of life.
I want you to laugh and play and discover who I am in the
midst of you."

We are called to be friends with others because Jesus wants us
to come closer and closer to *him*. Jesus wants us to know that he
is loyal to us; he's got our back. He wants us to know that his love
enables us to reach out to strangers and bring them to the table.

"I have called you friends," he says, so that we will know
that, when it's ten o'clock at night and something we dread has
happened, we can ask Jesus Christ, "Can you come?" And his
answer will be, "Of course. I am your friend."

---

5.   C. S. Lewis, *The Four Loves* (New York: Harcourt Brace Jovanovich, 1960), 103.

GREAT LOVE

"No one has greater love than this, to lay down one's life for one's friends."

—John 15:13

On September 11, 2001, we saw the best and the worst of human behavior. We saw what can happen when you "know" you are right. We saw what can happen when a cause overtakes all other considerations. The fiery determination to have our own way, to insist that the world is what we say it is, can push us to see every man and woman as simply a means to our end. Others become mere passengers on our private journey.

Such fanaticism is death. It's like the fanaticism of Ahab in *Moby Dick*, who searches for the whale beyond all reason, beyond all limits. He doesn't listen to the other seamen; he forgets the purpose of his voyage. Ahab thinks only of the one white whale, yet his fanaticism prevents him even from seeing the whale for what it is. For Ahab, the whale is no longer a mammal, no longer a leviathan, no longer even a valuable commodity. For Ahab, the whale is evil and must be killed.

Ahab's shortsightedness pushes his world into the whirlpool of the sea, just as the fanaticism of the terrorists pulled the World Trade Center towers down in a heap. We saw the worst of human behavior: slaughter of the innocent.

And yet . . . and yet, we also saw the best. We saw open hearts and open arms. We saw men and women extend themselves for complete strangers, give their lives for people they had never met before. We saw people help others down the stairs of the World Trade Center only to be trapped themselves; we saw three hundred firemen rush into the flaming building and never come out; we saw the men and women on United Flight 93 choose to crash their plane rather than let more lives be taken. "No one has greater love than this, to lay down one's life for one's friends."

On 9/11 we learned that our friends can be people we have never met: men and women in an office building high above the street or in airplanes high above the ground.

In this time of *kairos*, deep time, we remembered what is best in the world. We remembered that life is very fragile and very precious, and for a time we remembered that we need one another. People all over this country and the world gave what they could: blood, time, medical supplies, money, tears, prayers.

At our best, we rediscover our common life; we rediscover that all of us are one body. We remember that what happens to you, happens to me. For a day, for a week, humanity's common pain and sorrow brought people into communion, into each other's arms.

I looked at pictures in the papers of people holding one another and thought to myself, "It's the *Pietà*, the mother holding her Son. It's Jesus being crucified again." Were you there? On 9/11, we were there, and we trembled, trembled, trembled.

The question is, having seen what we have seen, what now? What do we do the day after and the day after that? Well, we remember. We remember what we have seen so that we can avoid the worst and embrace the best. We remember that the only thing that matters is love: the Great Love that binds us to God, to our best selves, and to one another. Nothing else lasts. The Temple in Jerusalem fell; the World Trade Center fell— sooner or later, all monuments fall. Only the love of God survives.

Therefore, we must treat everything else with penultimate seriousness. Fifty years ago, theologian Herbert Butterfield wrote, "Hold to Christ, and for the rest, be totally uncommitted."[1] He meant that only God is God. God is the only absolute, the only one worthy of worship. If we hold on to anything else, sooner or later we will be the ones to crash. We will be the ones to slaughter the innocents.

After the crucifixion, the disciples were frightened. Some hid, some ran away, some probably embraced a new cause— any cause—to fill the hole in their hearts. But a few, like Mary Magdalene, felt the Great Love in their hearts and looked for their Lord. They followed their love down into the darkness of the place of death to look for him.

Mary Magdalene didn't care about a cause, and she didn't care about a movement. She just wanted to touch her Lord one more time. So she went into the rubble and asked the first person she saw, "Sir, if you know where they have laid him, tell me." If she had been in New York, she would have put his picture on telephone poles. She would have asked every fireman, "Have you seen him? Have you seen him?"

The Great Love keeps our hearts open, keeps us from worshiping a cause. When we remember the Great Love, we remember that life is precious. On that one day in September, 2,795 precious lives were lost. Life is God's first gift to us, and we are charged to revere it and protect it. We saw the agony in the faces of the bereaved as they walked up and down the streets looking for their loved ones. Those were not American faces, nor even ethnic faces. Caucasian, Asian, African, Hispanic—they were

---

1. Quoted in Douglas John Hall, *The Future of the Church* (Toronto: United Church Publishing, 1989), 87.

all the same face, the face of human sorrow. On 9/11 we learned in the ache of our hearts that *we do not want to see that face again.* Anywhere. Life is too precious.

Despite our pain and sorrow and anger and distress, let us remember who we are at our best. As Christians, we are people of hope. We are the people who have walked in darkness but have seen a great light. Because we have been touched by the Great Love, we refuse to despair. We have a vision of another way to live, where the lion and the lamb lie down together, where Christian, Jew, and Arab find harmony with one another, where swords are beaten into plowshares. Our Lord has brought us out of the house of fear into the house of love and commanded us not to go back.

On September 11, 2001, we saw the best and the worst of human behavior. In the days and months and years to come, we will have to choose between the two. Which way will we go?

HOME

"Do not fear! Here is your God. . . . He will come and save you."

—Isaiah 35:4

When my son Arthur was five years old, he went for his first weekend away to visit his aunt in North Carolina. Now his aunt was no stranger to him and he had been to her house many times, but he had never stayed away from his mother and me. We drove him up there with two suitcases: one with clothes and the other with toys. My wife and I thought: this can't miss. A lake, a swimming pool, horses, big-screen TV—a kid's paradise.

The next day the phone rang. "Hello," I said. At first there was silence. Then came those words that break your heart, "Can I come home?"

Can we all come home? That's the question each of us carries around somewhere in our hearts. We can be five or fifty-two; it doesn't matter the age or place. The human condition is

65

to be homesick. We are homesick for all that is lost and for all that could be. We are homesick for those we love but see no longer. We are homesick for that childhood world that is stable and safe. We are homesick for a world where only good things happen to good people. We are homesick for all that is promised, yet has not come to pass: a world of justice and mercy and peace; a world where all God's children flourish; a world we used to dream of before we knew what we know. Can we come home?

Homesickness is part of being human. It's in our spiritual DNA. It's not a new thing. We know it existed in the Isaiah's time. The Israelites waited and wandered so long for home, forty years in the desert. Then, just when this land was becoming home, the Babylonians captured Jerusalem in 586 B.C. They destroyed the Temple, the very center of home, and sent the Israelites into exile.

Now the Israelites were strangers in a strange land. They sat by the River Babylon homesick. The men and women told their children stories of Jerusalem and the Temple. They remembered all that they had and all that they lost and longed for a homecoming. Even the children longed to return to a home they never had.

In the midst of this time of dislocation, this time of heartbreak, Isaiah had a vision of going home. Isaiah knew that his people, like all people, live in the time of in-between. It's a time when you have lost what you had and not yet received what you have been promised. You are stuck at your aunt's house with your toys and stuffed animals. You hold on to things that help you remember where you belong and you hold on to the promise that one day soon you'll be taken home.

In a time of exile, which is where we always live, we live between memory and promise. We live between what was and what will be. We live with that longing to be home.

Frederick Buechner helps us go deeper into this idea of being homesick. He writes, "We carry inside us a *vision* of wholeness that we sense is our true home."[1] Home is not a place. Home is not a building. Home is not even a family or group of people. Home is a vision of wholeness. Being home is knowing that you belong and that you are connected to the One who is your home.

Home is finally tasting the kingdom of God—a kingdom where, as Isaiah dreams, "the eyes of the blind are opened, the ears of the deaf are unstopped, the lame leap like deer and there are streams in the desert." Home is where God's will is done on earth as in heaven. That's what we long for—the realm of God—the realm of peace and justice and mercy.

We are homesick because the inequities of our affluent world push us far from home. Isaiah is not dreaming of getting back to the house his grandfather left in Jerusalem. He is dreaming of a time when all God's children have houses. He is dreaming of a time when the deserts in our hearts are filled with the living water of God's love.

If you have not read Karen Hankins's book, *Teaching Through the Storm*, you ought to. She calls it *A Journal of Hope*, and it is, but I call it *A Journal of Homesickness*. She begins by telling of a fall afternoon in her first-grade classroom. Two girls, Meg and Clarissa, were working on a class mural. Meg was painting flowers and Clarissa was adding cotton balls to some sheep. Before she started painting, Meg told Karen that she wanted to take her shoes off because her grandmother brought them to her from France and she didn't want "drippies" on them. Karen Hankins writes that the shoes were indeed beautiful.

After the girls worked a while, Clarissa came over and held up two cotton balls. "Can I have these to take home if they be left over?" she asked. "I guess so," Karen said. "Are you going to

---

1. Frederick Buechner, *The Longing for Home* (New York: HarperCollins, 1996), 110.

make something with them?" "No, I am going to put them in my ears at night to keep the roaches out when I be sleeping."[2]

We are not home until Clarissa can sleep without cotton balls. If our hearts are open, it doesn't matter what our individual houses look like. We will be homesick until the gap between Meg and Clarissa narrows.

The good news is this: like Isaiah and like all God's children, we have a memory and we have a promise. Jesus knew we would feel homesick. Therefore, he said to us what he said to the disciples before the cross took their home away: "I know you will miss me, so when you feel homesick, do this in order to be home with me. Drink the wine, eat the bread, and you will remember home."

Then he promised that one day we would all eat again together. One day we will sit at the table with Isaiah and Jesus and all the company of heaven. Remembering home in the past and remembering the promise of home in the future allows us to have glimpses of home right now.

I did get in the car and drive five hours up and five hours back to bring Arthur home. When he came into the house, he wandered around reclaiming his world. "My room," he declared. "My cat, my bed, my home." That night, he asked me, "Dad, I won't have to leave home again, will I?" All I could say was, "I don't know, Arthur. I don't know." But of course, I do know: we will all be homesick.

As I write this, Arthur is an ocean away and someone else lives in that house in Nashville. Some days he's homesick and so am I, and so are you. But I also know this: in this in-between time where all passes, we hold on to the promise that one day God will bring all of us home. Yet, even as we long for that day, we have glimpses. We have moments when we taste the bread of heaven and the kingdom draws near.

---

2. Karen Hankins, *Teaching Through the Storm* (New York: Teachers' College Press, 2003), 5.

Can we come home? "Yes, yes, yes," Jesus says, "come home. It will take a lifetime, but if you travel with me, I'll be your home both then and now."

HOSPITALITY

Do not neglect to show hospitality to strangers, for by doing that some have entertained angels without knowing it.

—Hebrews 13:2

Do you remember that song from *My Fair Lady* that asks, "Why can't a woman be more like a man?" I wonder how often we unconsciously sing our own version: "Why can't other people be just like me?"

There is a part of us that distrusts difference. We categorize and categorize, and our world grows smaller and smaller. Why can't other people be just like me?

In the Greek myth, Narcissus falls in love with his own reflection in the water. He becomes so enamored of himself that he finally tumbles into the water and drowns. There is a part of each of us that is narcissistic. That part of me wants to be around only white, middle-class, Southern men who are Episcopalian, like UNC basketball, read mystery novels, and are liberal in their politics. That's who I want to hang out with. Like Narcissus, we are looking for people who look "just like me"— and we drown in our idolization of ourselves.

Scripture gives us a very different view. Hospitality is a virtue and, like all virtues, it must be practiced. In the Letter to the Hebrews we are told, "Do not neglect to show hospitality to strangers, for by doing that some have entertained angels without knowing it." In like manner, Jesus calls on us not to surround ourselves with our relatives or rich neighbors but to invite in the people we normally see as discards: the poor, the crippled, the lame, the blind. Instead of insulating ourselves from difference, we are to invite the stranger into our lives. How are we to do that? What does it mean to be hospitable? Let me make three suggestions: be open, be honest, and look for Christ.

The Greek root of the word "hospitality" is *hospes*, which means "guest." We are able to welcome the guest only when we recognize that we are all guests. We have the illusion that we own our houses or land, that we possess our children, or that we control our lives, but all of that is idolatry, worshiping our own ego. Life is grace. Everything that happens to us is a gift. "The Lord gives and the Lord takes away. Blessed be the name of the Lord."

So long as we think we are in control, we cannot be hospitable, because when a stranger comes to the door, we ask ourselves whether this person is intruding on our lives rather than whether God is doing something in this place. In Deuteronomy, Moses tells the Israelites, "You shall also love the stranger, for you were strangers in the land of Egypt" (Deuteronomy 10:19). Disruption teaches us about being guests.

When I was twelve years old, my family went on vacation to Florida and stayed on a ranch about an hour from Gainesville. The second day there, my father got stung by a bee and went into anaphylactic shock. We dragged him into the car and sped to Gainesville, where he was in the hospital for a week. My brother, sister, mother, and I had only the clothes on our backs. My mother had even forgotten her purse. We stayed in a Howard Johnson's and went to the hospital to wait. I remember how much simple acts of kindness meant: helping us get clothes, bringing my mother coffee, showing us kids where we could swim.

We have all been strangers in the land of Egypt at one time or another. When we remember those times, then the stranger in front of us is us. We are all guests. Catholic priest and spirituality writer Henri Nouwen says, "Poverty makes a good host." The more we have to defend, the less hospitable we can be. Have you ever been to someone's house where you were afraid to touch anything? You sit on the edge of the chair and sort of hold your breath. We cannot be good hosts if we value our things more than another person. So first, we need to open.

Hospitality is not about providing an empty space, it's about entering into a relationship with someone else. When we invite someone into our homes, we allow them to enter our lives. When we baptize someone into the body of Christ, we don't say to them, "the Church is whatever you want it to be." We say, "These are the things we hold as important; this is what we believe as Christians. We invite you to be part of this, knowing that we will be changed by you, just as you will be changed by us." That's why hospitality is so scary: it demands being honest and open with someone else. Our inability to be hospitable makes many of our connections with people superficial or antiseptic. A real host says to the guest, "I think enough of you to let you know who I am and what I believe." We need to be honest.

Finally, to be hospitable, we need to change the way we look at the stranger. We extend hospitality because that is how we stay alive. Without the stranger, I become Narcissus and drown in myself. However, the stranger is not just the one who adds difference to our lives. The mystery of hospitality is deeper.

St. Benedict's Rule, a guide for monks written in the sixth century and still used today, says this about welcoming strangers to the monastery: "All guests who present themselves are to be welcomed as Christ, for he himself will say, 'I was a stranger and you welcomed me.' . . . All humility should be shown in addressing a guest on arrival. . . . By a bow of the head or by a complete prostration of the body, Christ is to be adored because he is indeed welcomed in them."

It's not just that we entertain angels without knowing it, we entertain Christ himself. Through the mystery of the Holy

Spirit, Christ is alive in this world. If we want to see him, we must look into the faces of other people. If we want to serve him, we must welcome the strangers into our homes and our lives. For if we do not, we worship ourselves.

When we feel that God is absent from our lives, it might be because we have narrowed our vision to the point of seeing nothing but ourselves. God calls for us to change the way we look at the world. When you go to a Benedictine monastery, the first thing the monk says to you is, "Your blessing, please." They know that God blesses us with strangers. God reveals Godself through the other.

Before he was called by God to rebuild the Church, St. Francis was something of a dandy. He loved nice things, and since his father was a wealthy cloth merchant, Francis always had fashionable and immaculate clothes. They lived in a nice house and associated with people much like themselves. As a young boy, Francis had a great fear of lepers. They epitomized for him all that was ugly and dirty in the world. He didn't want to look at them and crossed the road to avoid them.

After his conversion, Francis took a vow of poverty. No longer did he have nice possessions to protect, and therefore he was hospitable to all people—except lepers. He still was deathly afraid of lepers. One day, Francis was walking through the streets of Assisi when a leper approached him. Francis's fear came back, but this time he steeled himself. Instead of crossing the street, he walked up to the leper and kissed his face that was covered with sores, and in that moment Francis felt the presence of Christ surround him. Francis peered into the stricken face of the leper and saw the face of Jesus Christ.

We can be like Narcissus and waste our lives worshiping ourselves. Or we can be open, honest, and embrace the stranger, believing that the face unlike our own is the face of our Lord.

IDOLATRY

> But God said to Jonah, "Is it right for you to be angry
> about the bush?" And he said, "Yes, angry enough to die."
>
> —Jonah 4:9

Woody Allen once said, "Either there is no God or He's
incredibly incompetent." Well, Jonah has never heard of
Woody Allen, but he knows all about God's incompetence.
Every time things are going right, God screws everything up.
Jonah has waited all his life to see Nineveh—the capital of the
Assyrians—get its just deserts. Finally, the day has come! The
writing is on the wall: those irritating, despicable Ninevites
have forty days until they are no more, and Jonah is marking
off the days on his calendar.

It's not just that he hates the Ninevites: their mere existence
means that there is no justice in the world, and Jonah is a man
who longs for fairness. Jonah wants to know that the good are
rewarded and the evil are punished. He wants a world that
makes some sense, that has some order. Otherwise, how can he
keep going on? If everyone mocks the rules and gets away with

it, what's the point of rules in the first place? Is God keeping score or not? Finally, finally, God is going to act sensibly.

Then, with forty days left to go, God begins to wimp out. "Jonah," God says, "Go to Nineveh and tell them to repent."

"What? You've got to be kidding me! You want me to go *where*?"

Jonah refuses to go, not just because he is stubborn (which he is), and not just because he hates the Ninevites (which he does). Jonah will not go because if God lets these people off the hook, then God is not worthy to be God. If God lets them off the hook, there is no order in the world. Right is wrong and wrong is right. Jonah would rather be in the belly of a whale than have his world turned upside down.

But turned upside down it is. Jonah delivers his message— in the most unemotional way possible—and the Ninevites repent. The scripture says God "changed his mind about the calamity that he had said he would bring upon them" (3:10). Jonah goes into a rage: "Lord, I knew you would wimp out! I knew you wouldn't carry through. I would rather die than live in a world that doesn't make sense!"

Most of the time, we are right there with Jonah. We don't want God; we want a bookkeeper. We want rigid fairness, not grace. We want to earn our salvation, and we want everyone who hasn't earned theirs to be damned.

Madeline L'Engle recalls an evening a long time ago when one of her small children was scared because a storm was raging outside the house. In the little girl's bedtime prayer, her petition was this: "Dear God, Please be God. Amen." That is a hard prayer to pray—to honestly, genuinely pray that God be God, because the hard truth is that God's ways are not our ways, and we almost always want to have our way.

We don't want God to be God because God's mercy irritates and offends us. We want God to take some parenting classes. Parents are supposed to say, "This is your last chance! If you don't straighten your room right now, you can't watch TV" . . . but God never sticks to the divine guns.

God doesn't make the last chance, the last chance. God never writes people off—even scuzzballs like the Ninevites. God invites them to repent, to return.

What would it be like for us to stop keeping score? Can we imagine God sending us to see some modern-day "Ninevites"? What if we went to see Timothy McVeigh? Or Saddam Hussein? Would we really want them to be spared and given the same eternal life we are given? Would we really want them sitting next to us, sharing in the body and blood of our Lord? Or would we feel like the workers in Matthew 20, who slaved all day only to see the latecomers get the same pay as they did? Can we pray the prayer of Madeline L'Engle's daughter, or is our real prayer more like, "Dear God, Please be like me"?

The great sin has always been idolatry: making God in our own image and then worshiping ourselves. How often we fall into that trap! As a result, try as we might, we keep getting religion wrong. We keep thinking that this Christianity thing or this God thing is about following rules. Robert Farrar Capon says, "If the world could have been saved by bookkeeping, it would have been saved by Moses, not Jesus. The law was just fine."[1] However, the world is never saved by bookkeeping. In a bookkeeping system, all we can do is white-knuckle it through life until we can relax in heaven. It's how you feel when you are studying for an exam while all the rest of your friends are driving around town and going to the movies and having fun. "Just wait," you say to yourself, "you'll get yours." There is part of us that rejoices when we get a 94 on the test and they get a 53. That's fair. That makes sense.

God, however, is only interested in love—and all's fair in love. Therefore, God invites all people—the losers and the ones with the lowest score possible—to open their hearts and feel the divine love so that they can love in return. That divine love

---

1. Robert Farrar Capon, *Parables of Judgment* (Grand Rapids, MI: Eerdmans, 1989), 56.

doesn't leave us on the shore with Jonah, sorry that God let the Ninevites off the hook. Instead, that love connects us to our brothers and sisters in Christ. When we are filled with God's love for us, it is too wonderful not to share, as when you read a great book or hear a wonderful piece of music or see a magnificent painting. You realize that you did nothing to earn this gift that the work of art gave to you, and the truth of that experience is so great, you want others to have it, too.

So, we have two choices. We can sit outside the party and mumble and mutter to ourselves about God inviting *those people* to the party. We can make a mental list of who ought to have been kicked out and a very short list of people like ourselves who deserve to be invited . . . but it takes a long time to make these lists, and by the time we finish, the party will have long been over.

Or we can choose the alternative and throw our lists up in the air. We can give up on making the world fair or just or sensible. We can get up off our duffs and realize that it's happy hour: the band is playing, the Ninevites are dancing, and everyone is having a ball, because they already know what we are just realizing: Jesus Christ has invited us to a party, and as long as he is going to be there, that's where we want to be, too.[2]

---

2. Ibid., 140–41.

JOY

Rejoice always.

—1 Thessalonians 5:16

When Paul says, "Rejoice always," we want to say, "Get real!" It sounds too good to be true, sort of like something out of *Mary Poppins*. Or it sounds too sweet, sort of like eating saccharine.

Of course, we can rejoice sometimes (at least when things go our way), and maybe, even when things aren't going our way, we can avoid looking miserable. But rejoice always?

It's especially hard to think about this during Advent. We already have a tendency to manufacture a festive façade in December. We decorate our houses—and we decorate our lives—so that we will fit in with the holiday cheer. To an extent, "Rejoice always" sounds like a command to stuff our real feelings away. But, despite our objections or reservations, there it is. Paul doesn't say, "Rejoice when you feel like it."

Rejoicing has to do with joy and, as a matter of fact, joy is embedded in the good news:

My soul magnifies the Lord, and my spirit rejoices in God my Savior (Luke 1:46–47).

I am bringing you good news of great joy for all the people: to you is born this day in the city of David a Savior. (Luke 2:10–11)

I have said these things to you so that my joy may be in you, and that your joy may be complete (John 15:11).

I tell you, you will weep and mourn, but the world will rejoice; you will have pain, but your pain will turn into joy (John 16:20).

The kingdom of heaven is like treasure hidden in a field, which someone found and hid; then in his joy he goes and sells all that he has and buys that field (Matthew 13:44).

Joy is a central component of the Christian life. But what is it exactly, and how can we experience it always? Well, I don't know whether I can define joy precisely, but I can name some of its attributes: joy is *constant*, joy is *creative*, and joy is *connective*.

Joy Is Constant

Joy is not really cheerfulness; it is not really happiness—at least not in the way we think about those things. We are cheerful or happy when life is going our way. But *joy* is our deep connection to God in Christ through the Holy Spirit. This is why joy is constant.

Paul is calling for us to be connected to God in our depths and not just on the surface. The love of Christ is the foundation of our existence, a gift freely given and always there, regardless of how our day is going. The love of Christ gives us the peace the world can never give and the world can never take away.

Joy is the lightness that comes from knowing that finally this is a benevolent universe. We know in our hearts that God is with us. In fact, it's even better: God is *for* us. Therefore, wherever we are, things are okay—even when they're not okay—because we know that God is in this world, moving it toward the kingdom.

Surely St. Francis was one of the most joyful of all the saints. I think this must be because he knew that, whatever happened, God would always be part of this world: Brother Sun, Sister Moon, we all are connected through the Creator. Therefore, Francis didn't have to make life work according to his will; it would work according to God's will. This isn't passivity, but acceptance. When we can be passive in this way, we can say, "Come, Lord Jesus," and live joyfully with whatever happens.

Joy Is Creative

Joy is constant. Joy is also creative. When we are joyful, we are free to play, because we have nothing to prove. Nothing we can do will make God love us any more, and nothing we can do will make God love us any less. Therefore, we are free to cast off our deadly seriousness and play in and with God's creation.

I remember a story of a young man who was tormented over what to do with his life. He went into the woods to pray, and he asked God over and over, "Should I go to school, or should I get a job?" Finally God answered, and the answer that came from on high was this: "*I don't care*! Just get on with it!"

It's not that God is indifferent; it's that we shouldn't take ourselves so seriously. We should take only God seriously. When St. Francis would come to a crossroads, he would spin himself around like a top, and whichever way he ended up facing was the direction he would take. The point is not to stop thinking about the direction of our lives; the point is to en-*joy* this life, to spin our lives around and around, confident that the Spirit of God is working in us.

When artists are at their best, it's as if the divine creativity runs through them. I think that's why artists, at their core, are joyful. But such creative joy is not limited to artists. God invites us to be joyfully playful in our attitude toward the world. The artist says to herself, "What if? What if I put that word or that color or that pose next to this one?" That "what if" echoes God's "what if": "What if the God-bearer is a woman from Nazareth without a husband? What if the Savior of the world comes as a carpenter's son from the edge of nowhere? What if I create a new heaven and a new earth?"

What if God's plan is true, and all our ways of thinking of the world are upside down? As followers of our Lord, we are called to be joyful, to insist that when the story looks like a tragedy, and all that can be seen is three crosses on a hill, the story isn't over. God still plays "What if?"

Joy Is Connective

Joy is constant. Joy is creative. Joy is also connective. Joy is the glue of the universe connecting us to God and to each other. It's infectious. We catch it from one another. There are certain people, the joyful people, that I just like to be around because my spirit is lifted in their presence.

There are other people, the deadly serious people, who make me feel like lead. In the face of deadly seriousness, joy says Christians and Muslims can love each other. Joy says there can be peace in the Middle East. Joy says there really is enough for every one, even if it looks like there are only two fish and five loaves.

Without joy, frankly, I don't know how else one could explain that weird gathering in some stable in the middle of nowhere. The young parents, the baby, the angels, odd towns-folk, and assorted barn animals—what an odd group! They didn't know one another. They had nothing in common, but joy bound them together. They looked at each other and laughed for joy. They looked at the baby and shouted, "Glory to God!"

The Christian journey is filled with unexpected turns. Our task is not to know where we are going, but to know that Christ is with us. That knowledge enables us to hear a voice whispering in our heart and soul, saying, "Wherever you are, high or low, glad or sad, God brings you tidings of great joy." Feel it. Follow it. Let it come into your heart and turn your life around. Let it pull you into a communion of joy. Let it free you to ask, "What if?"

JUDGMENT

Unless you repent, you will all perish.

—Luke 13:3

As soon as kids discover one magic word—"why"—conversations are never the same. "Why do we eat with knives and forks? Why do we have to wear socks? Why does Daddy get so mad when North Carolina loses at basketball?"

In a certain respect, we never grow out of that. We just ask about different things. Why? Why? Why did all those people suffer from the earthquakes in India? Why did those particular school children in California get shot in their school? Why this tragedy or that? Why?

Does the world make sense or not? If it does, then what is the explanation for so many horrible events? Why do they happen? If it doesn't, then do any rules apply? Can we do whatever we want with impunity? Is there any order to the world, or is this a random universe?

Jesus half answers our questions. He points to two tragic events: Pilate kills some Galileans and mixes their blood with the blood of sacrificed animals, and in another instance eighteen people are killed when a tower falls on them. Then he asks his listeners, "Do you think these events occurred because these were bad people?"

Did the people in India suffer because they deserved it? Did the teenagers in California deserve to die?

"No," he says. No. *No.*

We do not live in a mechanical universe, and—thank God—we do not get what we deserve. God is not the divine Santa Claus doling out candy or coal. God is not a divine clockmaker who has set the world going and then stepped aside. It may be tempting to think of the world like this, but we do so at our own peril because it turns our lives into a contest of works righteousness and eliminates grace. If God is the divine accountant or scorekeeper, then Jesus has gotten the Beatitudes all wrong. They should read,

> Blessed are those who never suffer, because that's how we know God loves them.
>
> Blessed are those who have no calamities, who never get sick, who are always in the right place at the right time, because they have earned their good fortune.

If God is the divine accountant, why does Jesus bother to help all these people? Don't they deserve what they get? This sort of thinking can't account for the crucifixion. Surely Jesus' suffering ought to end the idea that those who suffer most are the worst sinners.

But if there isn't an orderly, tit-for-tat scheme of things, where does that leave us? In a relative universe? Can we do whatever we want?

Well, no. Just because the universe isn't mechanical doesn't mean that actions have no consequences. There are always the two hands of God: the hand of grace and the hand of judgment. And the truth is, we know nothing about the either of those hands. We are like Moses asking for God's name and getting the hard-to-interpret reply of "I am" or "I am becoming who I am" or "I am the one who will be." In other words, don't ask. Just take off your shoes and listen.

That's what Jesus says as well: "Stop asking questions about how it works and look at your own lives. Instead of worrying about all those other folks, what about yourselves? Life is precious and time is short; now is the time to repent, to turn away from what is false and embrace what is true."

If we do not repent, we will be like a fig tree that has not born fruit in three years; that is, we will be half alive, half human. We will be going through the motions of life instead of living. If God thought like an accountant, then God would just cut us down, because a fig tree planted in a vineyard is just soaking up water that the grapes could use. The fig tree is just taking and taking and taking without ever giving back.

Jesus announces that there is both grace and judgment. God is not a bean counter, but God is also not indifferent. Instead, God is coaxing us, scolding us, begging us to turn around, for two reasons. First, because we are missing so much. The punishment for sin is sin. God doesn't need to punish us further, because sin cuts us off from experiencing the love of God. How could we be punished any more? In Dante's *Inferno*, those who are damned because they are angry are condemned to be angry forever. Those damned for lust are condemned to be lustful forever. The punishment for sin is sin.

Jesus urges us to repent because a life of sin is such a waste—it's a fig tree without fruit. It's a life without love or communion or grace. It's a ghostlike existence in which we fall down and worship some false god that gives us death instead of life. To repent is to remember what life is about and to turn toward it.

The second reason for repentance is that we live in time. I have no concept of Judgment Day, but I do know about time and how short it is. Think of loved ones in your life who have died, and think of all the words left unsaid. All the small acts you put off doing because you always thought there was time: the vacation you never took together, the conversation you always knew you'd have. . . . Think of your youth and all the dreams that are still just dreams. The fruit you thought you would bear but never did. If you have children, think of all the hours you spent at work when you could have been with them— hours you can never get back. We do not live in a mechanical universe, but there is judgment. Actions have consequences.

Because we are free, we are free to refuse God's loving grace or open to it. The good news is that God is not some mechanical agent of judgment. God does not hold up the scales blindfolded. Instead, God will do all God can to lure us into grace and life. If we choose, we can choose a hellish life. It's always our choice. As the divine judgment falls upon us, so do the tears of God. God weeps over our condition and, up until our death, God does all God can do to turn us around.

JUSTICE

> But let justice roll down like waters, and righteousness like an ever-flowing stream.
>
> —Amos 5:24

No one chooses to be a prophet. Who would want that job? You have to speak the word God has given you, but no one wants to hear what you have to say. In fact, they get sort of angry when you say it.

No one chooses to be a prophet. Instead, God chooses men and women, gives them the word, and then sends them to speak. That's what happened to Amos. He was minding his own business, breeding sheep and dressing sycamore trees in Judah, the Southern Kingdom, when God chose him and told him to go to the Northern Kingdom, Israel, and speak. So, Amos went to Israel and announced that he was a prophet sent with God's word.

At first, the people were excited. They wanted to hear someone who was "spiritual." They invited Amos to the Temple. To get in the right mood, they lit candles and turned on Gregorian chant. They were hoping he'd be as good as Henri Nouwen or maybe even Frederick Buechner. They sold tickets and T-shirts and were planning to tape his talks and sell them, too. The night of the performance, the Temple was crammed. They even had a downlink all over Israel so everyone could participate. The service began. Everyone held hands and sang "Kumbaya." Then Amos came to the microphone and spoke.

"You faithful people say you want the Day of the Lord to come, but do you know what you are saying? Do you think God cares only about your worship services? Do you think that following the Book of Common Prayer is all there is? Do you think that God cares only about church? Think again!

"Instead of looking at yourself, look at the world around you. Why are there so many poor in a country so rich? Why do so few have so much and so many have so little? Why do the powerful live in comfort and the powerless suffer?

"The word God speaks is this: 'You think you want the Day of the Lord, but think again!

'In the day of the Lord, the tables will turn. Justice will come rolling down like waters. Those who have thirsted will drink, and those who have been drinking will drown.'"

The hall was silent. No one clapped. No one asked questions. Everyone just left. Finally, the priest came up to Amos and invited him to go back to Judah. And that's how the story ends.

We don't know what happened to Amos. We don't really know what the Israelites did with his message. We do know that forty years later, Israel was conquered by the Assyrians. Its cities were destroyed, and its people sent into exile. Was that a consequence of Amos's unheeded warning? We don't know.

But we do know that Amos's words make us squirm, just as they made the Israelites squirm. Being a prophet is still an under-appreciated profession. But let's listen to Amos, even though what he says is not what we really want to hear, even though he, like all prophets, is calling for us to change in radical ways.

Amos's message is this: God intends justice. But we would much rather talk about charity than justice. *Charity* occurs when the rich decide to share some of their wealth with the poor. We prefer to talk about charity because it allows those of us with money to stay in control. We can decide when to give and to whom. In addition, talking about charity reminds us of how generous we are.

However, charity does not significantly lessen the number of people who still have less tomorrow or next week. I read a fascinating but very troubling book called *Sweet Charity*.[1] The author claims that the function of charity in America is not to bring fairness, but to act "as a sort of moral safety valve." Charity helps the one person in front of us but doesn't touch the inequities in our world. Charity helps us deal with a crisis but does little to prevent the crisis from occurring again and again. Charity means that we talk about hunger but not about poverty.

Justice is not about generosity. Justice is about fairness. The question justice asks is not "How do we help the poor?" but "Why do we have so many poor people?" It's a scary question. Dom Helder Camara, the Roman Catholic Archbishop of Brazil, said, "When I give food to the poor, they call me a saint. When I ask why the poor have no food, they call me a communist."

When Amos talks about justice, he has two things to say. The first is that we are interconnected: what happens to you happens to me. God intends for all people to experience a holy communion. Holy communion means "I can never be what I am supposed to be as long as others are not what they are supposed to be. You, too, can't be what you are supposed to be before I become what I am meant to be . . . That's just how the world is made. . . ."[2] The job of the prophet is to make us notice the people we have overlooked and pay attention to what people have and don't have.

---

1. Janet Poppendick, *Sweet Charity: Emergency Food and the End of Entitlement* (New York: Viking, 1998).

2. Dorothee Soelle, *The Silent Cry* (Minneapolis: Fortress Press, 2001), 277.

If we reduced the world's population to one hundred people:

Six people would have 50 percent of the wealth.
Eighty would live in substandard housing.
Seventy people would be unable to read.
Fifty would suffer from malnutrition.
One would have a college education.

What would the figures be if we focused just on the United States? Or just on our state? Or our county?

The second thing Amos tells us is to build fairness into our social and political infrastructure, so that justice will happen regardless of whether or not we are feeling charitable. Israel did, in fact, have such structures; Amos's job was to remind the people of what was already in place. God had told the people, "When you reap the harvest of your land, you shall not reap to the very edges of your field, or gather the gleanings of your harvest; you shall leave them for the poor." And every fiftieth year was a Jubilee Year: all debts were wiped clean, land was redistributed, everyone started over. Amos tells the people that they have disobeyed what is built into the law.

Now, we don't have an agricultural society like ancient Israel's, and we don't have Jubilee. We will have to dream up structures for our own day and time. It seems like an overwhelming task, but that's why we have God. After all, God gave the Israelites the structures they had, and God will give us ours if we pay attention and listen. Our job is to look for a new way and not resign ourselves to the way things are. Our job is to remember what kind of world it is that God intends.

Amos knew the Israelites had forgotten God's dream of justice, so he warned them that God would bring darkness, not light. What about us? What will the Day of the Lord look like for our world?

KAIROS

"Mary has chosen the better part, which will not be taken
away from her."

—Luke 10:42

Mary and Martha—we know what this story is about, don't
we? In fact, we know it so well that we all know which sister
we are, don't we? And if you're a Martha, like I am, you probably dread what's coming next. It's just not fair that Mary gets
the gold star. I mean, she really doesn't do much . . . how hard
is it to sit? Especially when there is so much work to be done
in the kitchen? Sitting around is all well and good until everyone gets hungry. I've even tried the Mary thing myself, as in,
"I'd like to help with the kids, but right now I need my quiet
time" or "I'd really like to help with the house, but right now
I need to get in touch with myself," but somehow I never get
a gold star.

The truth is, the way we have dealt with the story means bad
times for us Marthas. The way we have dealt with the story

means we are always going to have a divide between action and contemplation, work and prayer, the inner and the outer, doing and being, and on and on. "Choosing the better part" still means they are *parts* and not a *whole*. But speaking as a Martha, I am unwilling to get beat over the head with this story. I do not want to hear Jesus say one more time, "Porter! Porter, you have way too much on your plate. Stop thinking about all the things on the list and just sit down and let life happen."

It's not that we Marthas of the world don't need to work on our spiritual side (well, okay, maybe "work" is not the best word here . . .). We do need to let go of our tendency to over plan, over manage, and just flat-out obsess, but that aspect of the story has been analyzed and analyzed and analyzed. Thomas Aquinas, Martin Luther, Paul Tillich . . . all the big guns have preached on it. We Marthas know what to do; we just have trouble doing it.

Maybe there's another way to look at the story that doesn't leave us with this divide. I think the key to the other way actually lies in another visit Jesus makes to Mary and Martha's house that is recounted not in Luke's gospel but in John's. John 12:3 tells us that "six days before the Passover" Jesus came to their house, and "Mary took a pound of costly perfume . . . anointed Jesus' feet, and wiped them with her hair." Then Judas Iscariot complains that the price of the perfume was money that could have been used for the poor, but Jesus says, "Leave her alone. She bought it so that she might keep it for the day of my burial. You always have the poor with you, but you do not always have me" (John 12:7–8).

On any other day, it would be a horrible or even immoral idea to spend a year's salary on perfume instead of the poor, akin to Imelda Marcos having three thousand pairs of shoes while so many people in the Philippines scrounge in landfills for food. On any other day, Judas would have a point. But the day Jesus comes into your house is not any day—it's *the day*. The day Jesus comes into your house, all rules are off. So, maybe the Mary and Martha story is not about work versus prayer or doing versus being. Maybe it's about knowing what time it is, knowing the difference between *chronos* and *kairos*.

In Greek, *chronos* refers to clock time, the inexorable turning of the wheel. In *chronos* we know that the supper bell is going to ring whether we are ready or not. The Marys of the world can have all the beatific vision they like, but no vision is going to cook the food or serve the meal. But *kairos* is when the clocks stop, and we find ourselves in what T. S. Eliot calls the "still point of the turning world." *Kairos* is when time stands still and a door opens into a deeper reality; *kairos* is when Jesus comes to your house or your street or your life.

I don't think this story is just about being overly busy or, more precisely, Martha isn't wrong every day—just *this* day. The one thing necessary is to know when Jesus has come and to respond properly. When Jesus comes, everything is turned upside down: water gets changed to wine, five thousand people get fed from five loaves and two fish, fishermen leave their families and their job. Martha should know this. Jesus has already raised her brother from the dead after four days in the tomb. When Jesus comes, we need to step outside the rules and regulations and roles, because all that matters is him.

Yes, some of us do need to be more like Mary, and yes, the duty of every Christian is to pray—every day. And yes, in a world of ten thousand gadgets and machines that keep us perpetually busy, we are all distracted and worried by many things. So the story is a call to change our ways, to blend the Mary and Martha in ourselves, but it's also about knowing the time. We live so often in *chronos* that we forget about *kairos*, but the day Jesus comes is the time to bask in his presence. Mary will cook and clean and serve tomorrow.

Mary knows what we must all learn. The day Jesus comes is not any day. It's the day you have a glimpse of the kingdom, the day when suddenly you see that your deepest longing is to let go of some deep anger or paint landscapes or sail the seas. The day Jesus comes is when you finally know in your head what you have always known in your heart. *Kairos* is the day you finally knew what you had to do.

The day Jesus comes is also the day when you know in your soul that God loves you, that the love that binds the world together binds the source of love to you, and in the midst of driving to work or brushing your teeth that love beckons you to open your heart and feel the deep-down goodness of belonging to God.

On the day Jesus comes, we all have good reason to cook dinner or balance the checkbook or mow the lawn or wash the clothes or drive to work or brush our teeth. But if we do, the moment will pass. We will get our gold stars for being productive, but our hearts and our lives will not be transformed. We will miss the moment of grace.

Jesus came to Mary and Martha's house unannounced, and he's coming that way to our house as well. Let us pray that we stop in our busy-ness and pay attention to him. Let us pray that we step out of *chronos* into *kairos* and receive what he has to give. Let us pray that we know the time.

KINDNESS

Be kind to one another, tenderhearted, forgiving one another, as God in Christ has forgiven you.

—Ephesians 4:32

St. Paul writes the Christians in Ephesus to teach them how to be Christians. He goes through a laundry list of things to do and things to avoid. After a while, it sounds as if he's describing the Boy Scout oath: "Give up stealing; share with the needy; no evil talk shall come out of your mouth. . . ." And so on. But then, he offers a deceptively simple summation: *Be kind to one another.*

That's it? Be kind? It sounds as if the goal of Christianity is to be nice, but before we make this too easy, let's look at what "kindness" means. Kindness could be defined as loyal or stead-fast love: I act kindly to you because we are bound together in covenant. My life is part of your life, and your life is part of mine, just as God is kind to people because of God's covenant with them. The Hebrew word usually translated "loving-kindness" is *chesed*: to hold on to another. The root word of *chesed* is "womb." Thus, an image of *chesed* is the connection between a parent and child: not an intellectual decision, but a primal bond. Parents aren't kind to their children because they know they will get something from them in return. Parents are kind to their children because they love them.

Acts of kindness come from our being connected to one another. Interestingly enough, the Greek word for "kindness" can also be translated as "useful." Acts of kindness are what is useful for the covenant, for building and maintaining a sense of community. They are useful and even necessary for grow-ing in faith.

How, then, does this understanding of the meaning of kind-ness shape our sense of being Christians? I think that if we took being kind to one another seriously, it would reorient our sense of who we are. This is how Paul begins: "Putting away false-hood, let all of us speak the truth to our neighbors, for we are members of one another" (Ephesians 4:25). That's right, *we are members of one another*.

To be a Christian is to be countercultural. Our culture is almost entirely need-based. What do *I* want? What satisfies *my* needs? We tend to look at everything as consumers—How will this fit into my lifestyle?—and God forbid that anything will be required of us, or that we will have to be in covenant with people different from us, to *attend* to them, to care for them, to be kind to them.

A need-based culture feeds the ego instead of the soul. Its goal is to separate people, to divide them into categories of who belongs and who doesn't, who is in and who is out. Too often that need-based, consumer mentality shapes how we see the Church, and so we shop for churches the way we shop for houses. We ask ourselves what we *like*, what we agree with, and when we no longer like our church, we shop some more.

But Paul is pointing to a bigger picture: as Christians, we are to live in love. As Christians, we perform acts of kindness because we desire what is useful for the other person to grow in love and faith. We are kind because we are called to imitate God's kindness, which means we must be attentive—attentive to who the other person is and attentive to who Christ is.

When we get angry—and we will get angry—we are to hold on to one another until we work it out. "Do not let the sun go down on your anger," Paul says. Do not hold on to your anger or demonize the other person; instead, take advantage of the moment to grow in love. Take advantage of conflicts to remember that the world is bigger than you.

In the film *Dead Man Walking*, Sister Helen tells the condemned man that she will be present at his execution. She says, "I'll be the face of love for you." That's kindness. We are called to be the face of Christ for one another and to look for the face of Christ in one another. We believe that there are no throwaway people. Everyone is important and deserving of attention, kindness, and a place in the kingdom.

Every denomination has some sort of convention when representatives gather to discuss the major issues of the day. Typically, these gatherings are a wonderful mix of God's children. Of course, they have their successes and failures, but I am a fan of these conventions because they are such a wonderful image of our calling and struggle to be Christians: to love those who are different from us, to pay attention to those who disagree with everything we have to say, to take the other side seriously.

The Church is one of the few places that has an open-door policy. I've heard that in Boca Raton, Florida, many apartment complexes will not admit tenants who own pickup trucks. That is our culture in microcosm: if you don't look like us, you don't belong. The Church is trying to say that we care for one another not because we look alike but because God loves all of us.

A legend about Judas says that, after the crucifixion, he was filled with despair and threw himself into a deep pit. He lay there alone for a long, long time. One day, he looked up and thought he saw a small light a long way off. Slowly, he climbed up and up out of the pit, toward the light. When he reached the top and climbed over the edge, he found himself in a small, upper room where eleven disciples and a rabbi sat at a table. The rabbi beckoned to Judas and said, "Come, join us. We have been waiting for you."

By God's grace we are members of one another. So, let us be kind to one another. Let us treat one another in ways that build up the body. Because Christ's love is so much greater than ours, Christ intends for each of us—you, and me, and people with pickup trucks and different ideas, and even Judas—to have a place in the kingdom. Because Christ is in covenant with each and every one of us, we have been called to be kind.

LOVE

> "This is my commandment, that you love one another as
> I have loved you."
>
> —John 15:12

"Love" is one of those words that can mean almost anything. We say it all the time, but do we have any idea of what it means? It's been used in so many ways. Remember that line from *Love Story*: "Love is never having to say you're sorry"? That's true only if your love lasts one evening. On the other hand, Plato said, "Love is a grave mental disease." I'll not comment on that one. Confucius does a little better: "To love a thing means wanting it to live."

It may be that we need a sabbatical from this word, because we use it in too many places and in too many different ways. We say, "I love my car"; "I love my children"; "I love that color on you"; "I love you to death." No wonder "love" is confusing for us, but maybe this is not new. I wonder if the disciples were also confused when Jesus said to them, "I give you a new commandment, that you love one another." Someone, my guess is Peter, probably said, "Wait a minute! How can you command anyone to love someone else?"

When I was about five years old my twin sister and I were having a difference of opinion, and I hit her in the stomach. Unfortunately, my uncle was standing behind me, and he wasn't too interested in hearing why my actions were justified. In a forceful voice he commanded, "You two behave yourselves and start loving one another!" At the time, I didn't feel great warmth for my sister, much less love, but I did force myself to treat her more civilly, at least when an adult was in the room. At age five, I didn't know that resisting the urge to wallop my sister was the beginning of love, but it is.

It is because despite what we may think, love is not a feeling. Love is an agent of our will. Jesus doesn't tell the disciples to feel love toward one another. If we wait until we *feel* warm and fuzzy toward the people we live with—let alone the people we can avoid—we may never love them. What we need to do is make ourselves act lovingly toward them, and eventually our hearts will catch up with our actions. As a Twelve-Step catch phrase says, "Fake it till you make it."

To love one another is to treat one another with kindness and mercy and compassion. Although Jesus is talking to the disciples in this passage, we know that this command is not just for them. Earlier he has said, "Love your enemies. Do good to those who hate you. Pick out the people who drive you nuts and act lovingly toward them. Not because you feel like it, not because you want to, but because I command you."

In our age of freedom, sometimes we forget who we are as Christians. We are not free agents: we are servants of our Master. We follow Jesus' commands because our desire is to please him. We follow his commandments because they are *his* commandments. The wonderful thing is that, by obeying his commandment to love, we discover his love for us. Through practicing love, Jesus comes among us. Paradoxically, although we might think we are loving for Jesus' sake, we find to our surprise that we are loving for our own sakes. Loving is what cracks open our shells. Works of kindness or mercy or forgiveness open us up and bring us out of our small egocentric world into communion with the Other.

Still, we are seldom willing to encounter the Other, seldom willing to take the first step. Jesus knows it is hard to love those whom we would rather keep at a distance. He knows it takes a commandment to get us even to try.

The dominant movement in our society is centrifugal. It's as if every institution has become like an amoeba that divides and divides and divides. Forty splinter churches have left the Episcopal Church. No wonder our country has thousands of Christian denominations. We disagree and divide. Left to our own sense of freedom, we will separate and separate and separate. No wonder Jesus has to command us to love one another.

We might think to ourselves, "Okay, this is hard. I really don't want to be nice to those people who are wrong about everything, but I guess I can do it if I have to." But the commandment is even harder than that: love one another *as I have loved you.*

Oh. Maybe it's not enough to refrain from hitting your sister. Maybe it's not even enough to be nice to the people who irritate you. Maybe that's why it's a *new* commandment. I wish the gospel were just about being nice. That's hard enough, but I could maybe do that. But the gospel means something deeper: being willing to extend ourselves for others; serving others for the sake of our Master. It means putting others first.

In his wonderful novel *The Assistant*, Bernard Malamud describes a very ordinary man named Morris. Morris is a grocer who has hired an assistant named Frank. Frank cannot understand why Morris goes out of his way to help other people so often: giving someone more food than they can afford to pay for; letting someone kicked out of his house sleep in the basement; hiring people that don't look as if they deserve to be hired. One day Frank asks Morris, "What do you suffer for, Morris?'

"I suffer for you," Morris says calmly.

"What do you mean?"

"I mean you suffer for me."[1]

As Christians, we are commanded to suffer with one another and for one another. It doesn't have to be heroic; often thinking in grandiose terms only lets us off the hook. Instead of waiting to go to Haiti or India, begin where you are. Who are the wounded people in your life? What part of yourself can you give to them to ease their pain? Who do you know who is in need of the simple gift of touch? Of kindness? Of remembering that they too are children of God? Who do you know who has lost hope, who believes there is never going to be an end to racism or sexism or the forces that divide us? How can you stretch yourself to give the gift? To speak the word? To suffer for them? Begin there and work your way into the Mother Teresa thing. Start with not hitting your sister and work outward. It's what the Master commands.

---

1. Bernard Malamud, *The Assistant* (New York: Farrar, Straus, & Cudahy, 1957), 125.

M

MYTH

"You may freely eat of every tree of the garden; but of the tree of the knowledge of good and evil you shall not eat, for in the day that you eat of it you shall die."

—Genesis 2:16–17

Myth is a mystery. Working with myth is like going to a play: it's an enchanted world where anything can happen and anyone can be anybody. As you become involved in the drama, you give your heart away to it and suspend your disbelief. But afterward, you start to wonder, "How did they do that?" and "What did it mean?" You go look behind the curtain and see the actors without costumes or makeup. You read academic books and learn that the playwright stole from other plays. Someone tells you that there are underlying meanings to the play that are less than noble. After all this, it's hard to return to sitting in the audience and giving your heart away to the story in the same way as before. You can't watch the play with the same eyes.

That's what's happened to the story of Adam and Eve. We know too much to be able to hear the story anymore—we just hear our interpretations of the story. Walter Brueggemann, the Old Testament scholar, lists some of these interpretations.[1] We think the story is about how evil came into the world, but the Hebrew scriptures offer no explanation of evil. The creation story is concerned not with how evil began but with our faithful response to it. Alternatively, we might think the story is about how death came into the world, but the story is more about anxiety and separation than death. Or, we think the story is about how sex and evil are intertwined, but this requires reading the snake as a sexual symbol and linking the humans' shame at their nakedness to shame about sex, when in fact the story doesn't say anything about sexuality. Finally, there are a slew of interpretations about how the male is dominant and the woman is the temptress. Elvis Presley had a song that starts, "Hard-headed woman / Soft-hearted man / Been causing trouble ever since the world began." But this interpretation misunderstands *adam* as a name rather than a Hebrew term meaning simply "earth creature." It takes the admonition that the male would rule over the woman out of the context of balance, equality, and mutuality that is evident in the series of curses. It sees God's final intention as one of estrangement, where the result of our disobedience is a world of control and domination.

Let's try wiping all these interpretations away for a moment. Let's pretend we're going to the theater for the first time and try to see what the story tells us about who we are as humans and about our relation to God. Brueggemann says we learn three lessons about our identity from this story.

First, we learn that, from the beginning, human beings have a vocation: God put the earth creature in the garden of Eden to till it and keep it. God intends that we share in God's work of caring for creation. Our calling, our work, pleases God and helps us grow into who we are. To be fully human is to embrace one's calling, one's way of participating in the divine work.

---

1.   Walter Brueggemann, *Genesis* (Atlanta: John Knox, 1982), 40–54.

Second, we learn that, from the beginning, humans have a permit: you may freely eat of all but one tree in the garden. As hard as it sometimes is, our freedom is a gift. The world is ours for better or for worse. The man and woman can go anywhere in the garden, and the abundance of food takes away their constant concern for survival. God's intention in creation is that people not be consumed with a sense of scarcity. Wealth is not to be hoarded and used for power and domination.

Finally, we learn that, from the beginning, humans have a prohibition: of the tree of knowledge of good and evil you shall not eat. Humans are limited. We live in obedience to God. Creating meaning always involves creating boundaries. As G. K. Chesterton once said, "When people lose faith, it's not that they don't believe in anything; they believe in everything."

Instead of being about the cause of evil or the domination of males or the origin of death, the creation story actually offers an anthropology, a picture of what it is to be human: humans are characterized by vocation, permission, and prohibition. To be fully human is to hold all three in balance: to work with God, to be without fear, to know limits.

The story of Adam and Eve tells us that in the beginning, human beings maintained this balance successfully, and because of that they were in harmony with one another (they were made of one flesh), with creation (they knew the names of all living things), and with God (they walked with God in the cool of the evening). But once one aspect of that harmony was upset, all relations went askew. They became alienated from God and estranged from one another, and they lost all that they had. They found that they resented prohibitions, and they perverted the permission to enjoy grace into a permission to put the self at the center—and they forgot their vocation. As a result, nothing came easy and they lived in fear.

Maybe we need to turn this story upside down. We usually talk about the fall in terms of what we have lost, and our explanations are about whose fault it is—it's the woman's fault; it's the snake's fault; it's God's fault. However, if we turn the story upside down, we can see it as a summons rather than a lament. The story doesn't just tell us about Adam and Eve's loss: it also tells us about what God intends for human beings and all of creation. As Paul says, "Just as by the one man's disobedience the many were made sinners, so by the one man's obedience the many will be made righteous" (Romans 5:19). Through the grace of Jesus Christ and the gift of the Holy Spirit, we are called to shed our shame and anxiety and separation and to embrace what was lost. We are called to remember God's intention for us as earth creatures. Why should we settle for the consequences of our fall as our permanent condition?

God never intended that we live by domination. Men are not meant to rule over women. The rich are not intended to rule over the poor, nor the strong over the weak. God's purpose is not for us to consume the earth but to cultivate it, to care for it. God never wanted us to live lives of license or to exercise unbridled freedom. God's intention is for us to have unbridled trust in God.

So let us see what can be regained. We can't go back to Eden, but we can strive for the kingdom and look for the new Jerusalem. Is the prime activity of life to be making money and living by the sweat of our brow? Or is our true vocation to restore the original harmony?

Are we to create a world in our own image, a world that we own? Are we really to believe that everything we have is the result of our own efforts? Are prohibitions simply hurdles to be overcome? Is the slogan for Outback Steakhouse true: "No rules. Just right"? Should we do whatever we want to just because we can? Or does obedience to God mean aligning our desires with God's desire? Novelist Walker Percy says that now we can do anything we like, but we have forgotten what is worth doing.

One legend relates that at creation, the first human asked God to trade places, and because the human asked and asked, God relented—but only for one second. However, once they had switched, the human refused to switch back, and the world has never been in right relation since. Instead, the universe has been filled with deep longing.

Our hearts will always contain that longing until we find the balance of vocation, permission, and prohibition and thereby find our rightful place.

NEWNESS

The LORD said to Moses, "Is the LORD's power limited?"

—Numbers 11:23

First, it was slavery.

"God, how could you let this happen? We are the chosen ones; we are your people. Remember the promises? Here we are in this God-forsaken place, in bondage. If you are God, then release us!"

So God did a new thing: God brought them Moses, and through Moses God brought the plagues. Through Moses God parted the Red Sea and the Israelites came out of slavery into freedom. God did a new thing, because God loved God's people.

Next, it was the desert.

"God, we ran out of Egypt with nothing—just the clothes on our backs. Now we are in this desert. Have you brought us out of Egypt just so we could starve?"

So God did a new thing: God sent them manna, bread from heaven that rained down from the sky, enough for every day.

No longer did they work to make bread for someone else to eat; they were fed by grace. God did a new thing, because God loved God's people.

Then, it was the food.

"Manna, manna, manna . . . we are sick of manna! What I wouldn't give for a burger! Remember the food in Egypt? Fruit salad . . . steak . . . shrimp . . . and beer."

So God did a new thing: God sent them quail, quail, and more quail. God sent them so much quail they got sick. God did a new thing, because God loved God's people.

After that, it was Moses not having enough help.

"I cannot do this by myself. I am tired of babysitting a whole nation of crybabies! God, you started this, and you need to help me."

So God did a new thing: God sent the Spirit into seventy Israelites, and they all began to prophesy.

But the problems and complaints didn't end there. There was Babylon; there was letting Gentiles into the Church; there was the Reformation; there was forming an American Episcopal church; there was the new Prayer Book; there was women's ordination. So God did all sorts of new things because God loves God's people.

We as the people of God are still whining and God is still doing new things. We get stuck and God responds. And while God can handle the stuckness, God could do without the whining. God's hope is that we will begin to look for newness instead of spinning down into negativity, that we will stop our whining and embrace the new thing. We live in the midst of miracles, yet we keep trying to go back to Egypt. We live in the midst of newness, yet we keep trying to confine God within our comfort level. Over and over, we try to make God into a golden calf instead of recognizing the God of newness. We do this in many ways, but I can count at least four:

First, like the Israelites, we can worship a past that never was—a golden age—and thereby keep from ever stepping into the present. It's like the joke: "How many Episcopalians does it take to change a light bulb?" "Change? Who said anything about change?" The truth is, we'd rather sit in the dark.

Next, we focus on the nonessentials to avoid acknowledging that anything is new. A friend of mine who is a priest told me that one couple left her church because one Sunday she preached from the aisle and not the pulpit. They were more concerned over where she stood than about what she said.

Third, we worship our rules and forget why they were given to us in the first place. I knew another priest who was so bothered by the acolytes playing with the torches and not putting them in the right place, perfectly symmetrical to the altar, that she nailed the holders to the floor and glued the torches into them.

Finally, we believe that we and only we have the truth, as if the truth were so small it could exist in only one place—which happens to be where we are. In the year 2000, the Roman Catholic Church came out with a statement asserting that salvation and redemption are only possible through the Roman Catholic Church. When I heard that, I wondered why it isn't enough to know that you have access through your denomination and pray that others have access through theirs.

However, we are seldom content with just being connected to Christ, who is the source of truth. Instead, part of us says, "For me to be right, you must be wrong." When the disciples come to Jesus and say, "Teacher, we saw someone casting out demons in your name, and we tried to stop him," Jesus says, "Whoever is not against us is for us" (Mark 9:38, 40). Because Jesus knows that God always brings newness and is not interested in or dissuaded by our foolish tactics of limitation. We can worship the past, focus on nonessentials, obsess about the rules, or monopolize the truth—but, you know what? It doesn't matter. God will continue to breathe the Spirit into the world, because God loves us. The Spirit that blew over the waters at the creation, the Spirit that blew into Amos and Micah and Jeremiah and all the prophets, the Spirit that blew into the Upper Room that night of Pentecost is the Spirit of newness.

The only question is this: Will we continue to whine, or will we open ourselves to see and embrace and participate in the newness that God always brings? If we can, then we can begin a new pattern, something like this:

Then the people became frustrated. They felt they were stuck, but instead of whining, they prayed: "O God, our help in ages past, our hope in years to come, deliver us. Blow your Spirit of newness upon us, and give us open hands and grateful hearts to receive the newness you bring."

OPENED

Then looking up to heaven, he sighed and said to him, "Ephphatha," that is, "Be opened."

—Mark 7:34

A long time ago I entered the third grade. Having completed two years of school, I sort of knew how I stacked up against the rest of my class. I was in the redbird reading group in SRA, which meant I wasn't the tops with the blue birds, but I wasn't a buzzard either.

So I walked into Mrs. Anderson's room that first day of third grade somewhat relaxed. However, things were not the same as they were in second grade. Instead of sitting in the front row, I sat in the back. For some reason, I couldn't get anything right. I couldn't even copy the multiplication tables correctly

Just when I began contemplating life as a third-grade dropout, Mrs. Anderson called my mother. I was certain I was being demoted, but my mother hung up and said, "Mrs. Anderson says you need glasses. Can you see?"

"Of course I can see," I said.

To the doctor we went. The first day I got my new glasses, I remember walking out of the office and looking up. I shouted, "Look, the trees have leaves!" It was like seeing the world for the first time. Instead of a world of blobs and fuzzy shapes, I was in a world of details.

Mark's gospel tells of Jesus' curing a man of his deafness and his speech impediment. Jesus puts his fingers in the man's ears. He spits on his hands and touches the man's tongue and says, "Ephphatha—Be opened," and the man is in a new world—a world of sounds, a world of interaction.

"Ephphatha—Be opened."

Our journey toward Jesus Christ is a process of opening up more and more to the reality that is all about us. As Christians, we are people who are waking up. We are waking up to see and hear that the risen Christ is part of our world. We are waking up to see and hear that God is transforming the world into God's kingdom. We are waking up to experience the grace that is all about us.

There is a story of the Buddha sitting with his disciples. Just as Jesus asks the disciples "Who do you think I am?" and they rattle off their profound answers, so does the Buddha with his disciples. Some say, "You are the Enlightened One" or "You are the Soul of Souls." Finally, the Buddha looks at them and says, "I am awake."

"Ephphatha—Be opened" is to wake up.

However, it's hard to wake up and to be opened. It's hard to know that there is another way of seeing and that there is another reality beyond this one. I didn't want to get glasses because I didn't think I could see any better. I assumed that everyone lived in a fuzzy world. I thought that was all there was.

We are often in that place. I have met so many people who are so sophisticated and cultured, yet they have never grown out of a childhood picture of God as an old man with a white beard sitting in a reclining chair somewhere in a place called heaven. They never awakened to the reality of God because they can't imagine other ways of thinking.

This is also true of the way we act toward one another. We don't hear the deepest cries of the person sitting next to us. We don't see their deepest needs. Instead, we see what we want to see, and we hear what we want to hear.

Be opened, but it's hard. Sometimes we have to be shaken out of our customary ways of seeing. Sometimes we have to be jarred awake. We have to be opened up.

I am fascinated why people react so strongly to certain events. Something happens, and it opens us up. An example is the death of Princess Diana. Why did that event transfix so many people around the world?

For me, it was simply the shock of death. I expected Mother Teresa's death but not Diana's. It didn't follow the plot of her life. It opened me up once more to just how fragile life is. It reminded me that we can be thirty-six years old and be a princess and be beautiful, but we are always mortal. Moreover, we are never in control.

Jesus is calling us to stop thinking we know what life means and to stop being on automatic all of the time. Instead, he calls us to step into the real drama of life: the drama of dying and rising with him over and over again.

He often calls people by shocking them into being opened. In Mark's account of the healing, Jesus is in Gentile territory. He is not in the Temple. He is not with the Jews. He is with the common folk: the riffraff of the first century.

As if that isn't shocking enough, he breaks a taboo. He spits on his hand and puts his hand on the man's tongue. To spit on someone is to defile him or her, but Jesus is not concerned with etiquette. He is concerned with opening us up to be with him. To be opened means to let go of our conceptions of the world, our prejudices, our ideologies, all the ways we have put God in a box, and see and taste what is.

God always wants to open our eyes and our hearts and our lives. Sometimes God pushes and sometimes God pulls. God shocks us just as Jesus did. The world suddenly brings us up short and we have to reexamine everything.

But sometimes we are pulled into a new vision. Sometimes we can turn a corner and be overwhelmed by the beauty of the world. We can be overwhelmed by the grace of our Creator. We walk along feeling unconnected to our surroundings, unconnected to other people, and unconnected to our deepest soul, and we look up and are embraced. Then we may see that, as Gerard Manley Hopkins says, "The world is charged with the grandeur of God / It will flame out like shook foil."

The truth is, as we walk along this journey of faith, we are constantly closing off to the mystery. However, because God never gives up on God's children, God will do whatever it takes to push or pull us into life. Regardless of our age and our reading group, in all places and times God reaches out the divine hand and says, "Be opened, Ephphatha."

P

PENTECOST

And suddenly from heaven there came a sound like the rush of a violent wind, and it filled the entire house where they were sitting.

—Acts 2:2

Do we have to sit next to the Elamites? They are such trouble-makers—always picking fights and criticizing people.

Well, I simply refuse to share the same space with those Parthianians. Look at the way they eat their food: wiping their hands on their shirts, licking their fingers, sucking on the bones. . . .

What about the Cretans? The name says it all. They are so dumb it's a wonder they could even find their way here.

When we forget Jesus, this is what happens. While Jesus was with the disciples, no one cared who came in or out. Every now and then someone would complain about the Gentiles or the women or the children, but it wasn't a big deal because they were next to Jesus. As long as they could see him and touch him and hear his voice, then who cared who else was there? They all knew that Jesus had no taste; they all knew that he would let anyone into the circle. The riffraff would come to him with their problems and the next thing you know, he had his hands on them and was healing them and inviting them to be with him.

Once in a while, Peter would come up with an idea: "We need to get organized! Now, I've made up a sample membership card for people to apply for. I'm thinking we can color code them: the red ones get you into public gatherings, like the feeding of the five thousand event; the blue are for your basic teaching sessions—Sermon on the Mount, etc.—but green . . . green is the hot ticket! Green cards get you into the exclusive events, like the Upper Room dinners."

Jesus would turn and look at him and Peter's voice would trail off, because as long as the Lord was there, who cared? The disciples knew it wouldn't last forever—Jesus kept telling them about the suffering and the three days and the rising again, and something about a Comforter—whatever that was—but no one thought about all that stuff when he was around. They only thought about him.

Then, one day it was over. Jesus came back for a little while, but then he ascended to heaven and there they were, left with all these people on their hands and not knowing what in the world to do with them. So long as he was there, who cared about different customs? Without him, though, those differences are all we talk about. We argue over ideology and fight over our little pieces of turf. It seems like all we do is define ourselves by who we are not.

Sometimes we remember the promise: "I will be with you and send you a Comforter. Just focus on me, because if you do, you will see my face in the faces of all people." But usually we forget.

When the Church loses its focus on Jesus, it is the Church at its worst, because it sees only the differences that plague us. When we forget Jesus, it is as if we are taken over by a centrifugal force that hurls everything outward and away.

Of course, the problem is everywhere, but I am most familiar with the divisive nature of the Episcopal Church. We had a wave of parishes splitting off from the church in the 1970s and 1980s, mainly over the revision of the Book of Common Prayer and the ordination of women. Now a new wave is looming over us because of the issue of homosexuality. At the 1999 triennial convention of the National Episcopal Church, two of the bishops announced that they would not receive the bread or wine in the Eucharist from any of the ninety bishops who signed a statement supporting the dignity of homosexuals. They no longer could see the face of Jesus Christ in those with whom they differ. I wish other denominations were immune from such divisions, but we live in a world of schism. It's as if the dominant force in the universe is centrifugal.

Of course, this centrifugal force is not just in the Church. In past centuries, cities had a common green, a place where the community gathered and shared their stories—a place of communion. Now we organize ourselves into protected communities and have zoning laws and homeowners' association regulations concerning whom we allow to be our neighbors. Our only common green is the television or—perhaps—the anonymous Internet. We structure our lives so that we don't have to deal with difference, and then we wonder why we are so lonely.

The truth is that we cannot find holy communion by ourselves, and we cannot find holy communion without the presence of Jesus Christ. Without Jesus, we may manage tolerance and respect of one another's rights, we may have coalitions, but we won't have *communion*. Communion comes only when the Spirit of Jesus unites us.

So let us remember the promise and how it came to pass. The reading from Acts says, "Suddenly from heaven there came a sound like the rush of a violent wind, and it filled the entire house where they were sitting" (Acts 2:2). That wind is the Holy Spirit, bringing Jesus back and blowing him into us so that we will never be separate from him again. On that day, Jesus suddenly was present again in the center of the room and in the center of people's hearts, uniting all the people once more. They looked at one another and saw not the differences but the face of Jesus Christ. In the Creed we say, "We believe in the Holy Spirit, the Lord, the giver of life." We know what that life is: "I am the way and the truth and the life." The Life comes from the Spirit and connects us to Christ.

So here we are, placed into a world of difference, in the middle of a Church with all sorts of voices, each claiming their rightness. We cannot will ourselves into a holy communion. We cannot make grace come. We can only open our doors and windows and be ready for the wind to blow through. We can only let go of our little agendas and our need to be right by making everyone else wrong. We can only pray for the Spirit to blow in our church, our lives, and our world, and refuse to settle for anything less than the life it brings. Let's remember the promise: the wind is always blowing—right here, right now.

On that day in that Upper Room so many years ago, everyone was arguing—the conservative bishops wouldn't sit with the liberal ones, but then the rush of wind came, and they all became very still . . . until an Elamite spoke, and then a Parthianian, and a Cretan, and soon everyone in the room was talking, and shouting, and singing in his or her own language. *But it wasn't noise.* It was the wind blowing through them, and when you listened closely, you could tell that all the tongues blended together to say, "Jesus Christ . . . Jesus Christ . . . Jesus Christ."

PRODIGAL

But we had to celebrate and rejoice, because this brother of yours was dead and has come to life; he was lost and has been found.

—Luke 15:32

One of the more popular theories about how families or organizations work is systems theory. In essence, it says that the various members of any unit take on specific roles that complement each other as parts of an integrated machine. Each of us performs a particular task in the organization and, as long as we follow the script, everything goes fine.

There are as many roles as there are people: the hero, the victim, the mascot, the patient, the clown, the consoler, the holder of anger, and so on. But two roles are ubiquitous: the hero and the screw-up. So, for example, one child is the hero—the perfect daughter who gets all As and is a star athlete. She gets voted "most popular" in the yearbook, and all the teachers love her.

Then there is the screw-up—the child who talks too defiantly, dresses too wildly, and doesn't do well in school. His teachers wring their hands and say, "Why can't you be more like your sister?"

The point is that we get locked into these roles, and we need everyone else to stay in their roles in order for us to stay in our spot. The hero needs the screw-up to stay a screw-up so that she'll look even better, and the screw-up needs the hero to stay a hero so that he won't have to compete. The system works as long as everyone stays put, but when someone starts rocking the boat, everyone gets nervous—because if one member changes, we all have to change. For example, in many alcoholic families, if one person gets sober, not everyone is happy about it (amazingly enough), because now they have to deal with a person they had written off a long time ago. Every family is a system, and every community is a system. One section of town is where the heroes live, and another section is where the screw-ups live—where the prodigals live—and as long as everyone stays put, all is well.

Of course, the good news Jesus has to proclaim is that God is moving people around. Through Jesus, God is announcing the good news that you don't have to stay put. Jesus begins his ministry by proclaiming the year of Jubilee, the year when everyone gets to move around. It's like the end of Halloween, when we all take off our masks and go to our real home. Perhaps with this in mind, we can hear the prodigal son story in a new way.

Once there was a family where all the members knew where they stood. The older son was very good. He obeyed all the rules, and everyone told him, "You are so good! Thank God you're not like your brother." Whenever the good son forgot who he was, he just remembered all the trouble his brother was in and then he knew: "Oh, yes. I know who I am: I am not my brother." He really didn't enjoy all the effort it took to be so good, but he knew that people expected it of him. He was afraid what would happen if he ever stopped. Who would he be without his merit badges? He was afraid that his father gave him love in exchange for his goodness. Without it, would his father even look his way?

The younger son wasn't bad, but nothing he did was right. It was almost to the point that he messed up simply because people expected it. They would laugh and shrug and say, "There he goes again." The problem was that, after a while, he had to get away. He thought for sure that he had messed up for so long and in so many ways that his father had no love left for him. He thought his brother had sucked up all the good deeds, all the good grades, all the good grace—so what did he have to lose?

When he left, no one knew what to do. The good brother didn't look quite as bright without the shadow of the younger brother. Now that they didn't have the younger brother's problems to discuss and remedy, the conversation around the dinner table came to a standstill. Suddenly they had all this time, and silence, and space.

The younger brother went far away to a place where no one knew him and no one expected anything of him. But he was alone. One day he had a memory of two small boys playing together. They were just children; back then, one wasn't right and one wasn't wrong. Their father came out and held them both in his arms and said, "I love you." He said it to both of them at the same time: "I love you." The younger brother remembered this and thought to himself, "I want to find that love again," and so he turned around and started walking toward home.

His father saw him coming from far away, and as soon as he saw him, the father knew that his son was not the same. He looked different. He *was* different. He was a new creation. His father suddenly knew that this was the day to give him a birthday party, because the son that had been stuck in being wrong was dead, and the real son finally had come home. His son.

So he threw an amazing party. Everyone was there. The father sent out invitations that read, "Everyone come! Today is the day to throw off your masks and move out of your roles. My son is a new creation. I am a new creation, and so are you!" People came from the projects and from the country club. Black and white, gay and straight, liberal and conservative.

The eldest son, however, would have none of it. He refused to come to the birthday party. "How can you forget about all those mistakes? What about the money he lost? What about the kind of life he has led?"

The father begged him to join the party. "We're starting all over—no right son; no wrong son; just brothers. . . . The brother you knew has died; come and meet your new brother!" But the elder brother could not step into newness, and so there he stood, unable to be in the present and unable to recreate the past.

Here's the truth: each of us has been both brothers at one time or another. Sometimes we find ourselves far from home, certain we can't do anything right, and sometimes we know we are tired from always having to be right, right, right. But the Father—the Father remembers who we really are. The Father remembers us not as wrong or right, but just as children. If we hold on to that memory, we will also remember that God is always throwing a party—a birthday bash—and longs for us to come.

QUESTIONS

They no longer dared to ask him another question.

—Luke 20:40

It's just a few days before the Passover. It's just a few days before the arrest and trial. Jesus' time is drawing to an end. The time with him is very short and very precious. Some Sadducees come to see him. By this time, everyone in Judah knows who Jesus is: miracle worker; famous healer; wise man. The one who raised the girl from the dead. The one who threw out the moneychangers. The one who came into the city with the people shouting and waving.

Some say he's the next Moses; some say he's Elijah; some say he is the messiah.

So here are these Sadducees, learned men and members of the branch of Judaism that does not believe in a resurrection after death. These Sadducees finally get to encounter Jesus. This is their moment; their time in the sun. Yet, this is what they say: "Teacher, if seven brothers die in succession and each marries the same woman, one after another, to whom is she married in heaven?"

Excuse me? Here they are before the Christ, the Anointed One, and this is the best they can do?

There is a Jewish saying: "Rake the muck this way; rake the muck that way. It's still muck. Meanwhile we could be stringing pearls for heaven." How often do we waste our time raking the muck instead of stringing pearls for heaven? How often do we waste our time playing word games instead of seeing the Christ right in front of us? I was thinking of how much of our conversations are a waste of time. We fill our hours with talk of Monica Lewinsky or Elian Gonzalez or Gary Condit or whatever the controversy du jour is instead of stringing pearls for heaven.

There's a character in Saul Bellow's *Henderson the Rain King* who says, "And I thought how I had boasted to my dear Lily how I loved reality. . . . But, oh unreality! Unreality, unreality! That has been my scheme for a troubled but eternal life."[1]

Well, let us ask ourselves if that is our scheme as well. Have we avoided the reality of questions that matter? Karl Barth, the great twentieth-century theologian, once said: "The Bible gives to every [person] and to every era answers to their questions as they deserve. We shall always find in it as much as we seek and no more."

Do we use our questions to keep Jesus at arm's length? Do we only seek to play Trivial Pursuit? Are we afraid of encountering the living Christ because we really don't want him in our lives?

It's clear in the gospels that Jesus has no time for those who merely want to play games. He has no patience with those who merely want to trick him or to use him to prove how smart or righteous or perfect they are. Usually those who waste his time don't come off very well. Indeed, after this exchange, Luke writes, "They no longer dared to ask him another question."

However, Jesus always has time for questions that are real. He always has time for those who are stringing pearls for

---

1. Saul Bellow, *Henderson the Rain King* (New York: Viking Press, 1959), 307.

heaven, because the questions deep in our hearts are what lead us into relationship with him. Jesus always has time for questions like this:

Can you heal my child?

I have demons that torment me and I can find no rest. Can you help me?

I have lost my way to the circle of life. Can you bring me back?

No one will come near me because they say I am unclean. Can you love someone like me?

When people offer these questions to Jesus, the answer he gives is not a slogan or a sound bite. The answer he gives is himself. When the Sadducees or the Pharisees ask Jesus their trick questions, they usually get parables, stories that will puzzle their minds and invite them to look at the world in a new way. However, when women and men bring Jesus their deepest yearnings, he connects them to the Source of life.

When genuine people come to him with genuine questions, he often doesn't say anything, but he touches; he encounters; he relates. He invites people to journey with him on the Way.

The Latin root of the word "question" means "to seek." It's where we get the word "quest." To ask a real question is to enter on a journey. It's to begin traveling on the Way. Jesus gets exasperated with the Sadducees simply because they aren't willing to leave the station. They just want to play games and stay right where they are. They aren't right or wrong; they are just wasting their lives. They are just raking the muck.

In *Letters to a Young Poet*, an aspiring poet from America wrote questions about writing poetry to the famous poet Rainer Maria Rilke in Germany. In one of his replies, Rilke writes, "Love the questions themselves as if they were locked rooms and like books written in a very foreign tongue; . . . Live the questions now. Perhaps you will then gradually, without noticing it, live along some distant day into the answer."[2]

Our deepest questions don't have simple answers. Instead, they are doors to the unknown newness. Jesus says, "I am the Way" because with him and through him we live our way into answers.

Today is the day that Jesus has come to the city. Today is the day Jesus has come to our city. The time is short, but it is our time. Time to bring our deepest questions to him, the questions for which we want a new answer. *Does God love me? Are we alone? Can people find Shalom?* The Sadducees cannot ask these questions because they think they already know the answers. Real questions are doorways to the journey to newness. We ask Jesus these questions because he is who he is. Jesus is the door to newness. He is the Way to new life.

He invites us to think of a new world: a world where the old rules do not apply. He invites the Sadducees to lay aside their stupid question and think of a new world in which the living and the dead are connected.

Now is the time. Do not think about what we can do but about what God can do. Remember what he said? "Ask and you will receive." How can we receive if we never ask?

---

2. Rainer Maria Rilke, *Letters to a Young Poet* (New York: Norton, 1934), 35.

R

RECONCILIATION

And now do not be distressed, or angry with yourselves, because you sold me here; for God sent me before you to preserve life.

—Genesis 45:5

When he says his name, they don't know what to say. When he says his name, a door opens that they thought they had nailed shut.

When he says his name, their minds fill with all sorts of terrors, because they remember what they did to him and realize that he has had years to think about his revenge. "I am your brother, Joseph, whom *you sold* into captivity."

The brothers stood there looking at Joseph. They were before him because they were accused of stealing, but they now are forced to confront their real offense of selling off their brother. Now, they know that this is payback time. The tables are turned, and they are sure that soon they will find themselves at the bottom of a deep pit.

If this story were about just any family, we know what would have happened. The bloodletting would have continued and the cycle of violence would have taken one casualty after another. *You hurt me; I'll hurt you. Don't get mad; get even.* How familiar this is to us! How often our world is trapped in the repetitive script of endless retribution, where everyone is defined by his or her past. *You are the one who hurt me, and that sums up who you are.* We cannot stop the cycle of vengeance because we cannot see the other in terms of what he or she can *become.* Ours is a world of clear labels—good or evil, friend or foe, victim or oppressor—and once the labels are on, they are on forever . . . and, conveniently, we don't even have to wait to be harmed by an opponent: we can write him off after one glance at his label.

When Joseph says his name, the brothers think they know what's coming—but a new thing happens. Amazingly, Joseph looks beyond his own life and his own hurts to the future that God has promised to his father and grandfather. Joseph sees that if those promises are to be fulfilled, he will have to let go of his hurt and anger and participate in God's plan. Joseph tells his brothers, "This isn't about me. If it were, you would starve. This is about God and the promises made to Jacob and Isaac and Abraham." Three times Joseph says to them, "God has sent me before you to preserve life. . . . God sent me before you to preserve for you a remnant on earth. . . . It was not you who sent me here, but God" (Genesis 45:5–8).

God is calling Joseph to love his way out of the land of violence and into the land of forgiveness, a place from which he can issue his brothers an invitation. Because Joseph knows he cannot force his brothers into this new land, he gives them enough provisions to last through the famine. They must be given no reason to fear him and no reason to fake their thankfulness. They must be free to love Joseph in return or to withdraw from him. Joseph, like all God's people, believes that love and forgiveness are contagious. His extravagant gesture brings new life to his family: his father Jacob's spirit revives, and he goes to see the son he thought was lost.

As long as the story is just *my* story, all I care about is *my* agenda. But Joseph, through the grace of God, lifts his vision beyond his private story and so catches a glimpse of God's story: the story of reconciliation, of bringing all people into communion. Joseph lets God work through him to mend the world.

Without God, we are stuck in an endless cycle of retribution, but with God, more is expected of us. Jesus tells the disciples, "If you are going to follow me, you are going to have to think bigger. So what if you are nice only to the people who are nice to you? Anyone can do that!

"More is expected of you. God expects you to see the world differently. Love your enemies. Bless those who curse you. Pray for those who abuse you.

"If you don't, how else is the world going to change? If you don't, who else is going to break the cycle of violence? If you don't, someone is going to starve when the famine comes . . . and if one starves, we all starve.

"If you kill your enemy, part of you dies, too. If you seek revenge, God's plan for the world gets delayed yet another day."

This, ultimately, is what the story of Joseph and his brothers means for us. More is expected. Family, friends, coworkers, and neighbors will hurt us, sometimes deeply, and we must be the ones to issue them an invitation to step into the newness of forgiveness. Sometimes this takes a long time. Sometimes we are in Egypt so long they don't even recognize us anymore. But the time *will* come, and we must pray that when it does, we will be ready to let God work through us to mend the world.

The way home always leads to a confrontation with our enemy, and we are always given a choice: we can punish our enemy and stay in Egypt, or we can invite our enemy into a new relationship and be reunited with the One who loves us both. We can either win the power game or save our souls. Not surprisingly, poetry expresses this best:

From the place where we are right,
flowers will never grow
in the spring.
The place where we are right
is hard and trampled
like a yard.
But doubts and loves
dig up the world
like a mole, a plow.
And a whisper will be heard in the place
where the ruined
house once stood.[1]

As long as we are right, no spring will come. We must let doubts about our rightness thaw our coldness so that God can turn over the hard, trampled ground of our hearts. This is the choice: fear or love; revenge or newness; the cycle of violence or the circle of reunion.

Whenever we face this choice, let us remember that just as God sent Joseph to his brothers, so God has sent Jesus to us— and the reassurance is the same: "You need not die. God has sent me to keep you alive." Once we hear those words, God prays that we, in turn, speak them to the world.

---

1. Yehuda Amichai, *Selected Poetry of Yehuda Amichai*, trans. Chana Bloch and Stephen Mitchell (Berkeley: University of California Press, 1996). Used by permission.

S

SALVATION

What we will be has not yet been revealed. What we do
know is this: when he is revealed, we will be like him.

—1 John 3:2

It was hot—the way only noon in Palestine is hot. The town
had shut down for the midday meal; people were seeking sanctuary from high sun. It was so bright you almost couldn't see.

She walked with her head down—not out of shame, for she
had already dealt with shame. She had spent her whole life
dealing with shame, but today it was the sun.

She didn't see him at first, but then she heard him call her
name: "Mary." She stopped and stared. *Who?*

"Mary."

And with that, she began to weep. She began to weep
because he alone knew her name. She turned and walked
toward him, looking into those eyes. He saw all the way through
her; he saw something in her that no other man had seen. He
drew her out of the midday sun and into the light of his face.
She knelt before him, grabbed his feet, and said, "Master."

On that day, the demons left her. On that day, she was no longer the woman people talked about behind her back. On that day, she became the one he said she was: Mary, Mary from Magdala. On that day, she began to follow him.

The passage from the First Letter of John contains one of the most amazing verses in scripture: "Beloved, we are God's children now; what we will be has not yet been revealed. What we do know is this: when he is revealed, we will be like him" (1 John 3:2).

Can we comprehend that? *We do know this: we will be like him.* Spread the news! Therapists are going to have to either go out of business or go back to school. Our destiny is not in our past but in our future. The secret to who we are is where we are going, not where we have been. We are being made into the likeness of Christ. *We will be like him.*

Meister Eckhart, the thirteenth-century mystic, wrote that Jesus says to us, "I became human for you. If you do not become God for me, you do me wrong." Becoming Godlike for Christ is our destiny—that's what we are made for. The freedom of grace is that we are neither confined nor defined by our past. It doesn't matter if, like Mary Magdalene, you have seven demons inside you or, like Saul of Tarsus, your job is to persecute Christians. Once you encounter Jesus Christ, a transformation begins. It's like a divine Polaroid photo: your true self gradually emerges from the amorphous background, and the more you become who God created you to be, the more Christlike you are. You go from being a motel for demons to being the first apostle to see the risen Christ. You go from being a first-century Robocop to being the chief evangelist for the faith. Find your true self and you find your true name: Saul becomes Paul.

How this happens is a mystery. God knows how God changes people, but God doesn't tell us how it's done. But, my guess is that *we become who we long to be.* At that scorching noontide, Mary Magdalene caught a vision of how Jesus saw her. She knew that he didn't see her simply as one possessed by demons, the object of the town gossip, someone to avoid. He didn't see her as disposable. He saw her as the mirror of himself, and in that he gave her a vision of the one she might become. Jesus believed in her, and because of that, she both believed in him and came to believe in herself. Jesus spoke her name so that she might discover that her name was the same as his. *We become who we long to be.*

The earliest theologians of the Church called Christianity the "School of Love," because its members' primary task is to teach one another what is worth desiring. They called this lesson "ordering the affections." What we pay attention to shapes who we are.

It's no surprise that in a consumer culture we are bombarded with images of products that we "need" to buy in order to become a successful material self. All these advertisements are telling us what to long for, what to pay attention to. I wonder if there is anywhere left on this planet that is free of television. You can't wait for an airplane or sit in a hospital waiting room or even go shopping at Wal-Mart without the box saying over and over again, "Pay attention to me, and I will tell you what to long for. Look at me, and I will show you all the things that you need."

It's no wonder we lose ourselves; no wonder we forget who we are and where we are going. Who can concentrate with the voice of consumerism squawking at you all the time? We start to think that we are our possessions, our diplomas, our accomplishments. We need to be reminded of who we are, and then we need to remind one another of who we are. We are children of God being transformed into the likeness of Jesus Christ.

I think of how I've been reminded: sometimes its an offhand comment, sometimes it's a line between the lines, but whenever I get confused and lost, whenever I forget who I am, God speaks through the voice of someone else and reminds me of what is worth longing for.

When I was in high school, I didn't know what I wanted to do when I grew up. Then one day my eleventh-grade English teacher passed me in the hall on her way to somewhere else and said, "You're such a good writer . . . Maybe you should think about teaching English."

Who, me? But as of that moment, I thought of myself in a new way. My horizon had changed; what I longed for had changed; I had changed.

God speaks to us and through us every day, sowing the seeds of the truth of who we are. We just need to take the time to listen and let the seeds grow in our hearts. I need to remind you of how precious you are in God's eyes and that your future is to dwell in the house of the Lord forever—and you need to remind me. Then we need to go into the world and tell all the amnesiacs who they are. We need to tell all those who have lost sight of the goal the amazing news: *We do know this: we will be like him.*

One day, you will be walking through town in the heat of noon, when it's so bright you almost can't see. You'll be walking with your head down, not thinking of much, when you'll hear a vaguely familiar voice saying something you can't quite make out. So you'll turn and ask, "Did you call me?" And the voice will reply, "Oh, I'm sorry, for a moment you looked like someone I know. For a moment I thought you were Jesus Christ."

And as you walk away, a question will bounce around in your brain. *Do I look like Jesus Christ? Do I look like Jesus?* Then the answer will come to you: *If I don't now, I will. I will.*

SUFFERING

> Then he began to teach them that the Son of Man must undergo great suffering.
>
> —Mark 8:31

There is no middle of the road for Peter. He either hits a home run or strikes out. In Mark's gospel, Jesus asks the disciples,

"Who do you say that I am?" and Peter gets it right. He beats everyone else to the punch and blurts out, "You are the Messiah." Therefore, when Jesus starts to teach the disciples about his coming suffering, Peter is smug. He is certain that he is the valedictorian . . . but something is wrong. Jesus is not following the script. Jesus says that he must "undergo great suffering, and be rejected . . . and be killed."

Didn't Peter just say that Jesus is the Messiah? Doesn't Jesus know what that means? Peter is thinking of victory and acclaim and big office suites; of respect and reputation. So he takes Jesus aside and tries to get him on the right page. He tells Jesus to forget this suffering stuff and go for the big time. And suddenly Peter is not the star pupil. Jesus rebukes him. "Get behind me, Satan!" Jesus says to him. "For you are setting your mind not on divine things but on human things. . . . If any want to become my followers, let them deny themselves and take up their cross and follow me" (Mark 8:33–34).

We, like Peter, have to learn that the road Jesus leads us on is not the worldly road of success and safety and ego inflation. Daniel Berrigan, the Roman Catholic writer and social activist, says, "If you want to follow Jesus, you had better look good on wood." Following Jesus is scary stuff. It is always about death and life. The way of discipleship leads to the cross, which is both individual and corporate. The cross is about the death of our false self: we are to be stripped bare until we find that all we have is faith. The cross is also about bearing one another's burdens: we deny ourselves for others, to bring in God's kingdom. That's the Christian journey. No wonder Peter wants to avoid it. We all do. As poet W. H. Auden has the Magi say, "The journey is long and we want our dinner."

Lent, the season before Easter, is a time to change destructive patterns. One of them I work on each year is my eating patterns. Each Lent I resolve: no more rich desserts and salty, greasy snacks. Goodbye Breyers® ice cream and Cheetos®. Recently, just as my Lenten resolve was beginning to waver, I saw an ad in a magazine for the Body Maximizer, which gives you "the workout without the work." The Body Maximizer is a belt that runs electric current into your body so that you can gain muscle tone and lose weight without even moving. Now *there's* an invention that should sell: it offers change without pain! It offers us discipleship without the cross.

That's what Jesus means when he says Peter's mind is not on divine things but on human things. To set our mind on human things is to think in terms of our present comforts and conditions. To set our mind on human things is to think only of ourselves. Of course, Peter cares about Jesus and doesn't like the idea of Jesus suffering. Who would? There is nothing redemptive about pain in and of itself, but Jesus doesn't say, "Go suffer for the sake of suffering." What Jesus says is, "Take up your cross and follow me." Suffering is only redemptive when our cross is The Cross.

We are called to take our cross to Calvary, to be like the thief hanging alongside Jesus, for Jesus' promise to him is also his promise to us: "Today you will be with me in Paradise" (Luke 23:43).

What happens when we let our crosses be Jesus' cross is that he takes away our fear. We find that in the midst of suffering, God is with us. In the midst of suffering, we find the peace that the world cannot give and the world cannot take away. Once we find that peace, we know that grace is all that matters, and our job is to help that peace spread throughout the world by showing people how unafraid we are.

So long as we are afraid, we are trapped in human things. Our only pursuits are for comfort, pleasure, and security. We are only willing to stretch to help others so long as we are not inconvenienced too much, and we become very calculating in how we extend ourselves. I want to make sure that you deserve my help and are appropriately grateful for my help and, most of all, I want to make sure that my help doesn't cost me too much and is noticed in the right ways. I think that's why we are so good at symbolic gestures but are often unwilling to change the way we live. I don't mind marching for a cause. I know I can donate one morning out of my life, but don't ask me to change my life. Don't ask me to give too much of myself.

Jesus is not talking about symbolic actions; Jesus is talking about discipleship, about leaving our nets and our families, all that keeps us safe and secure—and stuck—and following him on the Way. We cannot be disciples if we are gripped by fear. We must encounter the love of God in Christ and be moved out of our fearful stuckness. Jesus moves our hearts so that we can move our feet. When that happens, then I am not afraid to help you carry the load, because I know that God is with us. I am not afraid to shoulder your burdens, because I know that experiencing the love of God matters more than being safe or comfortable or feeling pleasure.

Taking up our cross and following Jesus means we know what is worth fighting for and we know that all fights have a cost. There is no real life without wounds; what matters is whether the wounds are redeemed. We will all suffer, and we can either suffer together or suffer alone. Will we see our suffering as a failure to live in accord with the ways of the world, or will we see suffering as the gateway to grace? Do we suffer following the world or following Jesus?

Peter makes a lot more mistakes before the end of the story: he jumps out of the boat and starts to sink; he refuses to let Jesus wash his feet; he denies Jesus in the garden. Let's face it, taking up our cross is a hard thing to learn. Our first instinct is to turn away and save our lives. However, at the end of the story, Peter dies in Rome as a martyr for the faith. It takes some time and it takes the descent of the Holy Spirit, but Peter finally turns from human things to divine things.

Suffering for Christ's sake isn't about giving up ice cream or junk food. It's not about losing weight with or without a workout. It is about losing our fear and becoming disciples. That move requires turning just as Peter turned. Instead of focusing on ourselves, we turn and look around us for all those who are broken or weary and in pain. Then we speak the words of consolation by saying, "No one can take away your pain, but I know someone who can redeem it. I will walk with you because I know someone who walks with us and leads us to a new place and a new life. He is the One I follow. His name is Jesus Christ."

T

TRANSFIGURATION

You will do well to be attentive to this as to a lamp shining in a dark place, until the day dawns and the morning star rises in your hearts.

—2 Peter 1:19

Many years ago, a friend of mine got married in an outdoor service on a bright and sunny day in June. I happened to be standing next to the groom's mother during the ceremony. As soon as the bride and groom began exchanging their vows, she began taking pictures with her Polaroid. After a few minutes, I felt an elbow in my ribs. I looked at her, and she began showing me pictures she had just taken. The wedding was still going on, but she had already started memorializing it. In fact, I think she became more enamored with her photos than with the event itself. We all have this human desire to stop time and stay in the high points of life.

That's where Peter is in the story of the transfiguration. Jesus takes him with John and James up the mountain to pray. This may not have seemed like a big deal at the beginning, since

Jesus observed a certain rhythm: when things got crazy he
was always sneaking off to pray. No doubt Peter and company
took their prayers seriously, but they probably weren't expecting fireworks.

But on this day, all of a sudden all heaven broke loose. Jesus
was covered with dazzling light as bright as a flash of light-
ning. The disciples saw him standing with Moses and Elijah,
talking about the future. Luke writes, "Peter and his companion were weighed down with sleep; but since they had stayed
awake, they saw his glory and the two men who stood with
him" (9:32).

For the first time in their lives, these three disciples are fully
awake. For a moment their vision sharpens, and they see
through the veil of the everyday into the divine reality—and
they are dazzled. It's true that the day before, Peter confessed
that Jesus was the Christ, but they weren't expecting this! And
so Peter does what we all want to do: he wants to take a Polaroid
to freeze-dry the moment. He wants to build three tabernacles
so he can have a museum. People will come from all over to see
this wonder and to hear Peter's account. He'll be on Letterman
and CNN. He can stay in this peak moment forever.

Of course, it doesn't work. It doesn't work because we live in
time. Sooner or later, we all come down off the mountain:
every honeymoon finally darkens, every summer ends. Jesus
knows what Peter doesn't know: the road off the mountain
leads to Jerusalem and Calvary, the tomb and the garden and
beyond. We can't stop the story at the good parts. We can't say,
"I've maxed out! I've gotten all the bliss I need for a lifetime."
Life is movement and growth and change, joy and sorrow. Jesus
offers us "abundant life," and that abundance is a strange blend
of peaks and valleys, transfiguration and crucifixion. To deny
one is to deny both—and not be fully alive.

In the film *Shadowlands*, C. S. Lewis has found out that his
wife, Joy, is dying. As a boy, Lewis had seen a part of England
called the Golden Valley and thought it was heaven, so he and
Joy go looking for it. When they find it, they have their own

mountaintop experience looking down at this glorious view of the English countryside. Lewis tells his wife, "I'm not waiting for anything new to happen. I'm here now; that's enough." Joy replies, "It's not going to last, Jack."

Jack doesn't want to talk about that. "Let's not spoil the moment," he says, but Joy says, "It doesn't spoil it. It makes it real. I'm going to die. And the pain then is part of the happiness now. That's the deal."

To be real, to be fully alive, we must have peaks and valleys, pain and sorrow, life and death. That's the deal. Once we recognize that and embrace the whole of life, then we discover that the transfiguration is not an event that we merely observe; it is something we experience. We don't *witness* the transfiguration, we are being transfigured, and our Lord is showing us how. Peter has a glimpse into the true nature of Jesus as the Christ, and that glimpse transforms Peter. Joy Lewis says, "the pain then is part of the happiness now," but we can also flip that around and say, "The happiness now will be part of the pain at Calvary."

In his second letter, Peter says that you will do well to be attentive to the event of the transfiguration "as to a lamp shining in a dark place, until the day dawns and the morning star rises in your hearts" (2 Peter 1:19). Peter has seen God's glory revealed, and that vision becomes a lamp shining in a dark place. This is what we call hope. Once we encounter the living Christ, we know that the light is inside us. Even when we deny our Lord three times, we do not despair: the love of Jesus Christ is in us and will always be in us, and because of that love, we are not afraid to come down off the mountain. The love of C. S. Lewis for Joy and she for him enabled them to face her death. What mattered was not maintaining a peak experience; what mattered is that they were with one another—always. Wherever the one was, that's where the other one wanted to be.

When Peter and James and John come down the mountain, they go with Jesus to Jerusalem; the flip side of the transfiguration is Calvary. Instead of Moses and Elijah on his right and left, there are two criminals. Instead of the voice of God saying,

"This is my Son, my chosen; listen to him!" there is only the crying of the women and the jeering of the soldiers.

Abundant life, or what we call the paschal mystery, is the pattern of death and resurrection. The pain then is part of the happiness now; the happiness now is part of the pain then. We are being transfigured as we see that God is in all of it, the highs and the lows. Whether the mountain is Mount Horeb or Calvary, whether we are bathed in light or hanging on the cross, God is there. The moments in light prepare us for the moments in darkness; the moments of darkness become bearable because of the moments of light. Only by embracing both are we fully alive, and only by being fully alive can we see Christ as he is and allow him into our hearts.

The gospel is not an account about someone else; it's about us, because it's a road map for the journey of faith. Jesus is inviting us to travel with him and with Peter and James and John. He is inviting us to be transfigured, to come into the light—not so that we can stay there forever in some safe, wonder-filled sanctuary, but so that we can bear to go into the darkness. The freedom of discipleship, of following our Lord, is this: once we listen to him, once we are bathed in the light of his love, then it doesn't matter where we have to go. A hill with three crosses, an empty tomb, Rome, Corinth, your hometown, wherever—we know that he is there. The pain then is part of the happiness now; the happiness now is part of the pain then. That's the deal.

TRUTH

"Everyone who belongs to the truth listens to my voice."
Pilate asked him, "What is truth?"

—John 18:37–38

Sometimes the text isn't the whole story but just the outline. For example, one of the most dramatic encounters in the

Gospels is between Jesus and Pilate, but John's account is somewhat skimpy on the details. The text tells us, "Then Pilate entered the headquarters again, summoned Jesus, and asked him, 'Are you the King of the Jews?'" (18:33). But that doesn't tell us enough. It doesn't help us get into the story. We have to practice what the Jews call *midrash* and fill in the blanks.

Pilate is the Roman governor of Judea. He is surrounded by all the best and brightest, the spin-doctors of the first century. But Pilate is tired: tired of politics; tired of this place; tired of himself. He knows that his best days are behind him, and if his career were going anywhere, he wouldn't be in this backwater. The real action is in Rome, not in this pagan capital of nowhere.

When he was young, everything was so clear. Everything made sense. But not now. Now it's all opinion, it's all "perspective" . . . whatever that means. And then they bring in this Jewish rabble-rouser.

Pilate is ready to squash him and get on with his day, but something gives him pause. There is something different about this guy. He isn't afraid of Pilate's power. He looks Pilate straight in the eye.

"Are you the King of the Jews?" Pilate asks him.

"Are you asking because you want to know or because other people said to?"

The question sets Pilate reeling. This man is talking to *me*— *not* to the governor, but to the human being . . . *me*. What do I want to know? Really know? And can this troublemaker tell me? Or is this just another fanatic winding up to make a speech?

So Pilate and Jesus skirmish. They play a first-century version of Twenty Questions until Pilate finally takes his chance and asks the question he has been waiting to ask since he lost his youthful certainty, the question that will cut through the spin-doctors and the power brokers. "What," he asks, "is truth?"

And Jesus stands silent. Jesus stands and looks into Pilate's eyes until the politician knows that Truth is in that silence. That Truth is too big for words. That Truth is less an idea than a place: you turn a corner and suddenly the world comes together; you blink your eyes and suddenly you see reality as it is, whole and complete; you find that Truth is the place where all creation coheres.

Jesus stands silent and invites Pilate into that place, and Pilate almost enters, but then the crowd begins to shout and the chief of staff says, "Governor, you have another appointment waiting"—and the moment is gone. Pilate declines his invitation to grace because he gets caught up in the everyday compromises of his life.

In the church calendar, the last Sunday of the church year is called "Christ the King Sunday." The next week begins Advent and a new year. It is hard for us to grasp what the image of Jesus as King means. "King" brings images of separation, of one who has power and of everyone else who doesn't. But Jesus tells Pilate, "My kingdom is not from this world. If my kingdom were from this world, my followers would be fighting to keep me from being handed over" (John 18:36).

Christ is the King because he is the one who holds the world together. Christ is the King because he is the Truth. But, like Pilate, it is hard for us to grasp a truth that large. Our world is so fragmented, and our truths are so small. The word "diabolical" literally means "to throw apart." We live in diabolical times, times when the big Truth has been thrown apart and people clutch passionately to little truths.

What is truth? Well, we know what it is not. In the film *Buffalo Bill*, one of the characters says, "Truth is whatever gets the most applause." But the real truth is not trendy, not what's in vogue. Unlike Pilate, Jesus isn't interested in any polls. The truth is an encounter with what is real.

Truth is also not something we control, not something we own. When we encounter the Truth, it's more like Jacob wrestling with the stranger: God gives us our divine name, but we never walk as easily again. Our life is no longer our own; we have undergone a radical reorientation. To avoid that radical reorientation, we define the truth as something that exists objectively outside of us, that we can consider. We equate truth with an issue: gun control, nuclear weapons, abortion, or whatever. But those are merely ways of keeping the One who is the Truth at arm's length. Those are merely ways of staying in control and avoiding an authentic encounter.

Jesus doesn't pronounce the Truth—Jesus *is* the Truth. Ultimate Truth is not a proposition or an ideology or a possession. The Truth is an encounter with the One who is real, and that encounter is always transformative.

When we encounter the Truth, something happens to us. Jesus comes into the presence of Peter and Andrew and says, "Leave your family and nets and follow me," and they step into the new not because they understand what is going on, not because they agree with the positions Jesus takes, but because a new reality has entered into their hearts.

After all, who among us understands this? Do we really know why God loves us the way God loves? Does anyone here understand the incredible reality of God becoming flesh and dwelling among us? Do we comprehend the kingdom Jesus brings? These all are part of a Truth too big for us to grasp. Instead of holding on to them, we are held by them. Like leaven, they get into us and we are never the same.

Alan Jones offers two images for this encounter with the Truth. He says it's like a betrothal and a pilgrimage.[1] We fall in love with the Truth and pledge to spend our lives committed to it. Jesus doesn't want us to agree with him; he wants us to fall in love with him and commit ourselves to putting him at the center of who we are. We do so knowing that marriage, like all life, is about change. Our understanding of who Jesus is and who God is *has* to change. Peter and Andrew have no idea what is ahead of them when they lay down their nets and follow Jesus—the miracles, the crucifixion, the resurrection, Rome, martyrdom—but they are wedded to the Truth, for better or for worse.

---

1. Alan Jones, *Living the Truth* (Cambridge: Cowley, 2000).

This is why the Truth is an invitation to go on pilgrimage. We do not comprehend the Truth but journey toward it. The Greek word for truth is *alethia*—from *a lethia*, meaning "without forgetfulness." In Greek mythology, the name of the river separating the land of the living from Hades is Lethe—it's the river of forgetfulness.

The Truth helps us remember who we are. We encounter Jesus and feel a deep acknowledgment of our true self, so we leave all that keeps us in a perpetual state of forgetfulness and follow him. When we journey toward Christ, we journey toward the truth of ourselves.

If we want to stay in control, we will hold on to an ideological Jesus. We will stay in our heads forever and keep Jesus the Christ at arm's length. But if we want to be held by the real Jesus, we will listen with our hearts to Jesus' words: "I am the way and the truth and the life"—and then leave everything and follow him.

UNBELIEF

"I believe; help my unbelief!"

—Mark 9:24

It's hard to watch your child suffer. You feel helpless. If there were a way to take her place, you would do it. But there is no way to bridge the gap between child and parent.

We meet a desperate parent in Mark's gospel. A father has a boy who has been possessed by a demon since childhood. The man is at the end of his rope and has run out of options. None of the disciples can do anything, so he brings the boy to Jesus.

"If you are able to do anything, have pity on us," he says.

"If you are able!" Jesus replies. "All things can be done for the one who believes."

Here the father is caught: he knows what the right answer is; he knows he is supposed to butter this rabbi up. He should say something like, "Oh, Good Master, I absolutely believe! There is no doubt in my mind. Even though I have gone to fifty-three other healers, I know you are the one!"

However, he can't say it. Maybe he knows that Jesus is different. Maybe he knows that more is on the line here than mas-
saging this healer's ego. Maybe he knows that Jesus is calling
him to look again at how he relates to the world and to God.

How often do we find ourselves in that place? We know
what we want to happen, but we aren't certain—absolutely certain—that it can happen. When Jesus tells us that all things can
be done for the one who believes, do we believe him? Or do we
feel caught, like this sick boy's father, wanting transformation
but doubting that it's possible?

The wonderful thing about this story is that the father
doesn't give the "right" answer; he just says what he can: "I
believe; help my unbelief!" and the boy is healed. A lifetime of
waiting and worrying is over.

So often we think in absolute terms: I either have faith or I
don't. But the opposite of faith is not doubt. In fact, doubt is the
catalyst for faith. Our doubts are what move us to new places
and cause us to dig deeper into our souls. The opposite of faith
is *indifference*; "hardness of heart" is the term Jesus uses.

Novelist Flannery O'Connor tells a story of a man who does
not know how to live in the place between absolute certainty
and absolute unbelief. He calls himself the Misfit. "Jesus was
the only One that ever raised the dead," the Misfit says, "and he
shouldn't have done it. He thrown everything off balance. If He
did what he said, then there's nothing to do but throw out
everything and follow Him, and if He didn't, then it's nothing
for you to do but enjoy the few minutes you got left the best
way you can—by killing someone or burning down his house
or doing some other meanness to him."[1]

It's all or nothing for the Misfit: either it's all true and you
become a true believer, or none of it's true and then you have

---

1. Flannery O'Connor, *A Good Man Is Hard to Find* (New York: Harcourt Brace
Jovanovich, 1955), 28.

license to do anything. But, like the father in the gospel story, the choice doesn't feel quite that clear for the Misfit. He says, "I wasn't there, so I can't say He didn't raise the dead. . . . If I had of been there I would of known and I wouldn't be like I am now."

Our journey in faith is just that: a journey. It's a process, which is why the earliest Christians called their movement "the Way." We cannot understand the mystery, so we often grab for some "proof" that isn't really available: the Shroud of Turin, or the Dead Sea Scrolls, or the apparitions in Fatima, or the declarations of the Jesus Seminar, or testimonials about near-death experiences.

But none of these help. Sooner or later each of us will find ourselves just where the father in the gospel is. We will feel as if part of our selves, or part of our families, or part of our community is dying, and we will want to hope that God can and will resurrect us and our world. We hear those words, "All things can be done for the one who believes," and we want to say whole-heartedly, "I believe"—but we may be unable to say that.

Before we despair, let's remember who God in Christ is. Our job is to say what we can and begin our walk in faith. Our job is to put our lives in relation to Jesus Christ and ask for our deepest desire. Our job is to say what is true for us in this place and in this time—"I believe; help my unbelief!"—and God will bring new life.

VISION

It is a question of a fair balance between your present abundance and their need.

—2 Corinthians 8:13–14

Paul had a vision. Once he saw it, it was all he saw. His vision took over his life and drove him to the ends of the earth. Paul's vision is this: Christ's love has no limits. If Christ could love someone like Paul, then he loved everyone, everywhere. Christ didn't just love Jews—or even Gentiles who lived in Judah. Christ loved everyone, everywhere: Macedonia, Ephesus, Philippi, Antioch, Rome.

Think about it—Greeks, Turks, Italians, Palestinians—all connected to each other. One Lord, one faith, one body of Christ. One family connected only by the radical love of Jesus Christ. Different languages, different customs, different countries, but one love. It's a vision that can change the world.

During his first visit with the Christians in Corinth, Paul told them his vision. He told the Corinthians that God had blessed them with many gifts: an absence of war, an abundance of money, a sense of power. However, he said, remember the vision: "One Lord, one faith, one body. The Christians in Jerusalem, who are your brothers and sisters, have no money and few possessions. In addition, they are also being persecuted. Therefore, because you are part of them and they are part of you, I want you to share what you have with them."

To his great pleasure, members of the church in Corinth agreed. "Okay," they said. "We will set aside a portion of our money every week to give to our brothers and sisters in Jerusalem."

"Great," Paul said. And then he went to Macedonia and told them of the vision. The Macedonians were not rich like the Corinthians, but they also caught the vision.

Paul's Second Letter to the Corinthians contains a sort of a report card. The Macedonians, who have very little, have given to the Jerusalem Christians in abundance. However, the Corinthians, who have vacation houses at the beach and just got a tax cut, haven't given anything. Instead, they have second thoughts.

"Why should we help those people?" They ask. "They could get jobs if they tried. It's not our fault they don't have any money. Anyway, they're not our problem. They don't even live here."

And so the vision almost died in Corinth. It was almost replaced by the old fears that have been with us since the Israelites were slaves in Egypt. Whenever the vision slips away, the old fears fill the vacuum and whisper the voices of isolation and death in our ears that say: "The world is a scary place and there isn't enough for everyone. If you don't take what you think you could need, you'll get left out." Their motto became: "You are on your own."

Therefore, Paul writes back and says, "You've lost the vision, so I'll say it again. Do not be afraid; Christ's love has no limits. I am not asking you to make yourselves poor so others can be rich. I am asking you for a fair balance."

A fair balance.

This notion has an ethical and spiritual dimension. The ethical is the most obvious. God wants all God's children to have what they need to flourish. If they are indeed our brothers and sisters, we must want that too. A fair balance doesn't mean we all have the same amount of money or possessions, but it does mean that there is a minimum that as Christians we insist that every person must have simply because he or she is a child of God.

Paul says to the Corinthians—"Remember the vision: one Lord, one faith, one body. Your brothers and sisters in Jerusalem are hungry. How can you not feed them? They are your brothers and sisters: one faith, one Lord, one body." As Christians we are not called to feel love toward our neighbors but to do love. It is our ethical obligation.

There is also a spiritual dimension. To reach a fair balance means I give some of what I have to you in order that I can in turn receive what you have to give to me. If I never open my hands to give, then I cannot receive and I cannot know what grace is. The Corinthians could not imagine what the Christians in Jerusalem could give to them. What could they receive from those people?

They thought of themselves as the haves and those unfortunate people in Jerusalem as the have-nots. Their fear was that if they gave away what they had, they would simply have less.

The fear kept them from thinking of what they might actually receive. The Corinthians needed to give away their excess so that they could receive the rich gifts from those Jesus calls the little ones. That's the poor: the people who cannot rely on their wealth and, therefore, they have to rely on God. Affluent Corinth needed to share its wealth with poor Jerusalem so that Jerusalem would share the riches of its faith with the spiritually impoverished Corinthians.

The Corinthians needed to make some space in their lives to receive grace. They were out of balance and needed to find a fair balance.

We know the vision caught. In 125 C.E. the philosopher Aristides described the Christians this way: "If they see a stranger, they bring him under their roof, and rejoice over him, as if it were their own brother, for they call themselves brethren, not after the flesh but after the spirit." Historical records show that by 250 C.E., the Church at Rome supported 1,500 needy persons. In 361 C.E., the Emperor Julian tried to stamp out Christianity, but he admitted, "The godless Galileans feed not only their poor but ours also."

The vision caught, but the vision can be lost. The troubles the Corinthians had with it aren't unique to them. Every age and every culture has to recapture the vision, because the voices of isolation and death are very persuasive.

I don't say this as an American who speaks in terms of our freedoms and rights. I don't dispute our right to do whatever we wish with our abundance. Instead, I write as a Christian who finds himself in the land of the Corinthians. I write as someone who is in sore need of catching the vision.

We all know the statistics about the radical division in wealth in our country and the astronomical division of wealth in our world. Everyone knows how far away we are from a fair balance. This is not a question of losing what we need to flourish. It's a question of a fair balance in the essentials for life: water and food; medical care and schools. It's a question of helping our brothers and sisters simply survive. It's a question of thereby saving our souls.

When I read Paul's letter, I knew he was writing to me, and I knew that he was telling me not to forget Jerusalem.

You know where that is, don't you? Jerusalem today is Haiti and the Congo. Jerusalem today is Liberia and Mexico. And Jerusalem today is in every city because Jerusalem is wherever God's children are in need.

Paul had a vision. The Macedonians caught it; the Corinthians finally caught it; the Philippians caught it. The only question worth asking is this: Have we?

WILDERNESS

And the Spirit immediately drove him out into the
wilderness.

—Mark 1:12

If you go to the grocery store in Lent, you find that this season
is a hard sell. There just isn't any market for hair shirts these
days. So the grocery stores skip Lent and go straight for Easter.
Long before Easter Sunday, they have their shelves stocked with
baskets and chocolate eggs and bunnies. But while the grocery
stores may know about what sells, they don't know about resurrection. They don't know that the only way to Easter leads
through Lent.

The road from Jesus' baptism to his ministry leads through
the wilderness. The wilderness of Lent is unavoidable: it is the
crucible for our convictions, the place to find out whether we
really believe the words we say. When Jesus is baptized by John,
the heavens are torn apart so that God and the world are one.
The Spirit descends upon him and a voice proclaims, "You are
my Son, the Beloved, with you I am well pleased" (Mark 1:11).

We might think that from here on out Jesus can just coast. After all, how do you top that? But the next line says the Spirit—that's right, the Spirit, not Satan—immediately drove him out into the wilderness. God sends Jesus into the wilderness to let the words he has heard sink into his bones. Jesus must wrestle with the tempter before he is ready to minister to the world. Otherwise, it's all just words, nice phrases. But what is it about wilderness that has the power to bring about these important changes in perspective, for Jesus and for us?

First, the wilderness is in-between. You enter the wilderness the day after you take a new job or close on a new house or announce your engagement—when you realize that you do not know what you have gotten yourself into. The children of Israel left their slavery in Egypt, but they did not go immediately into the Promised Land. First, they wandered for forty years in an in-between land.

God is able to work on us when we are in-between because we are open and our defenses are down. It's easy to say we believe in God when the heavens are opening, the dove is descending, and the voice is crying out that we are the Beloved, but how about when we are on the road? How about when a stranger comes and says, "I've been where you're going, and it ain't so good. Are you sure you want to do this?"

The Lenten road is to Calvary. Let's be clear about that. We enter the wilderness when we realize that being a Christian means more than being nice and being affirmed, that being a Christian means that we, too, have to die before we are resurrected. We could stay at the River Jordan and sing "Jesus Loves Me" all day long, but if we are to grow up, sooner or later we have to move out. That's when we realize that this game is for keeps. It's not about the warm fuzzies. It's about dying so that we can be raised. Remember the end of *Dead Man Walking*? The condemned man says to Sister Helen, "I didn't know I had to die in order to love." That is what we learn in the wilderness, when we are in-between.

Second, the wilderness is where we are without other people. Yes, you are part of a body, part of a community, but no one can embrace the Truth for you. You cannot be saved by proxy. The wilderness is where we are forced to admit our real beliefs: Do I really believe that God exists and is for me? Do I believe the last will be first? Do I trust that this really is a benevolent universe, or do I spend my time protecting myself? Do I look for Christ in all persons, or are people a means to an end for me? Do I have faith that I am God's Beloved because of my baptism, or do I think I must prove my worth over and over again?

God does not want our words. God wants our hearts. Lent is a time to be alone and see where we are—where we truly are. Henry David Thoreau went to Walden to discover what he thought. He had to remove himself from society to find a foundation for his life.

Peter Shaffer's play, *Equus*, tells the story of a deeply disturbed young man who, because he is confused about who his God is, blinds six horses with a metal spike and winds up in therapy. Whenever the therapist asks him a question, he answers with a jingle from television. He sings out, "Double Diamonds works wonders, Works wonders, works wonders. Double Diamonds works wonders, So have one today!"[1]

The wilderness is a time to get away from mass-produced culture, a time to put aside all the slogans than have infiltrated our consciousness and find out who we are. Above all else, Christianity is an encounter. At some point or at some place, we meet God in Christ. No one can have that experience for us. Literally, "to believe" means "to be held by" or "to be grasped by." Our faith, as we proclaim in the Nicene Creed, is that we are grasped by God; we are grasped by Jesus Christ; we are grasped by the Holy Spirit.

In order for that to happen, we must go into the wilderness. We must make time and space to encounter the living God. Without that encounter, Christianity is all empty words and empty actions. One of the early Desert Fathers went to his

---

1. Peter Shaffer, *Equus* (London, Andre Deutsch, 1973), 22.

abbot and asked him for a good word. The abbot answered, "Go and sit in your cell, and your cell will teach you everything." We are to find our cell—our desert, our wilderness—and see what it has to teach us.

Finally, the wilderness is a place where we lose our carefully constructed clarity. In Nathaniel Hawthorne's *The Scarlet Letter*, the priest Arthur Dimmesdale has his life worked out—as long as he is in the town. As long as he is within the town limits, he knows the rules and he knows what his role is. However, when he and Hester wander into the forest, suddenly he enters the mess of his heart. He finds himself in a tangled web where he must wrestle with what he feels and with what he has done. That's the wilderness: a place not outside us but within us. God is calling for us to admit our confusions and confront them, because the journey of faith is not about being right, it's about being real. We cannot grow until we are honest about what we can affirm and what we cannot. This is why Jesus is so harsh when he condemns the hypocrites. God can't work with them hidden under their veneer of piety.

Lent begins when we admit we do not know everything, we do not understand everything, and maybe we do not believe everything, but we are willing to walk with God through the desert. The good news is that the angels ministered to Jesus in the wilderness, and they will minister to us as well.

Yes, the wilderness is an in-between place, a place where we are cut off from others, and a place of confusion, but it is also a holy place. It's the place we all have to go if we are to find new life with our Lord.

WISDOM

Wisdom has built her house,
she has hewn her seven pillars.

—Proverbs 9:1

Proverbs describes a character called Woman Wisdom. It's no accident that Wisdom is a *she*, because the writer of Proverbs is describing Sophia, who is a different kind of wisdom. Sophia is a feminine way of knowing. Most of the time we think of wisdom in more masculine terms: logical explanations, universal answers, absolutes. Our image of wisdom is the bearded man on the mountaintop, who ascends above the mundane to some great, abstract truth.

Sophia, however, is different. Sophia is a wisdom that focuses on particulars and is able to dwell in the confusing, contradictory world in which we live. For example, at Jesus' birth, the shepherds are visited by the angels who sing of the miracle that is to occur, and when they reach Bethlehem, they tell Mary these things. Luke writes, "Mary treasured all these words and pondered them in her heart" (Luke 2:19). That's Sophia: not to jump to any global answers or universal propositions, but to ponder the mystery in the heart, to let *what is* seep into the soul. Robert Frost wrote, "We dance round in a ring and suppose / But the secret sits in the middle and knows."[2] Sophia is the wisdom that enables us to sit in the middle and know, to treasure events instead of analyze them. She is what John Keats described as negative capability: a willingness to be with complexity and allow a certain messiness. As Jesus says, "Abide in me" (John 15:4).

When Jesus explains to the disciples what he means by "abide in me," he doesn't use any warm and fuzzy images. He doesn't say, "I am the good shepherd" or "I am the vine" or "I am the way." His language actually takes them aback: "Those who eat my flesh and drink my blood abide in me and I in them" (John 6:56). The disciples probably want to say, "Really, Jesus, a metaphor would probably work better here. Flesh? Blood? That's just too graphic." Plus, there is an underlying

---

2. Robert Frost, "The Secret Sits," *The Poetry of Robert Frost* (New York: Holt Reinhart & Winston, 1969), 362.

religious problem with his words: the law forbids Jews from consuming any blood whatsoever. The life principle, or *nephesh*, is in the blood, and thus it is a sin for a human being—a being filled with *nephesh*—to consume the *nephesh* of beasts, much less the *nephesh* of another person. This is why the Orthodox Jews soak meat in water for thirty minutes, salt it, let it stand for an hour, and then rinse it again— to draw out all the residual blood before it is cooked. So, when Jesus gives such concrete imagery, he makes things hard for the disciples—and hard for us. We don't want to drink blood or eat human flesh. We want our religion neat and logical and abstract.

Once a priest was instructing some parish children on First Communion and trying to explain that the bread was the body of Christ. One boy raised his hand and asked, "Is it his whole body?"

The priest, knowing he was in trouble, tentatively nodded his head. The boy pressed for clarification. "You mean his *bottom*, too?" That's the scandal of the incarnation. If the Word became flesh and dwells among us, then to know Jesus we must encounter the world—all of the world, even the messy parts. We must eat the flesh and drink the blood.

It is tempting to keep Christianity as a purely mental activity. We would prefer to think about "the cosmic Christ" as a sort of life force or anonymous energy field. There is always part of us that wants a sanitized Jesus or a privatized Jesus made in our image of what is holy—that nice man with the beard who is always sweet and who spouts off universal truths while sitting on a mountaintop.

Another temptation is to make Christianity into a set of rules or a list of causes or prohibited behaviors. Over and over we see the temptation to let the church give us simple solutions for complex problems. But look at the gospels. The Pharisees are always asking Jesus to give them yes-or-no answers, and Jesus is always telling them parables instead.

If we focus only on abstractions or rules, we can just stay in our heads about Jesus and never get down to the radical implications of the Incarnation. Never have to eat the gospel. Never have to take the good news inside us so it becomes part of the mess of our lives. Therefore, we will never know what faith, real faith, is. We have so much *religion* and so little *faith*. Faith is not about being certain; faith is about surrendering to a God who is moving in our lives in surprising ways—astonishing ways that lead us further into the mess of the world. Christianity is not just a mental activity. It is an encounter with the Word made flesh. Jesus didn't say, "Think nice thoughts and I'll be with you." He didn't say, "Just memorize these rules." He said, "You must eat my flesh and drink my blood." Eating flesh and drinking blood requires us to ponder in our hearts the mystery and the mess.

The wisdom of holy communion is Sophia wisdom. Sophia pushes us into the world and forces us deal with the incarnate Christ—the living Christ. The banquet that Christ lays, the banquet that Sophia lays, is not in our souls. It is found in relation to other people, in the messiness of the world. It's found when someone hurts us, and we have to resist our temptation to run away and instead go and work it out. It's found when we stop labeling those who are poor as lazy and see them as children of God. It's found when we keep faith even in the face of suffering, when we finally tear our scripts up for how we want the world to work and embrace the mess that is. It's found in the adventure of being embraced by a living God. Our world, our complicated, illogical lives, our mess . . . all of it is the flesh and blood of Christ. And if we want him, we must grab hold of our messy lives and eat.

WORK

Now such persons we command and exhort in the Lord Jesus Christ to do their work quietly and to earn their own living.

—2 Thessalonians 3:12

The Letter to the Thessalonians is filled with land mines—
especially the passages on work. There are so many ways to mis-
interpret them. They can be used to bash our welfare system or
to justify a lack of concern for the poor. We can use them to justify workaholism. How many times have parents wanted to say
to their kids, "The Bible says if you don't work, you don't eat"?

The land mines, however, lie less in the passages and more
in us, because most of the time, we do not have an adequate
understanding of work: it's either too important or not important enough.

When work is not important enough, it's only a means to an
end. We suffer forty hours for the sake of the other 128. I got
my first job when I was fifteen. I worked in the shipping
department of my father's sweater factory. At first the idea of
having a job was great, but after a short time—a very short
time—the glow faded. I had to get up way too early and the
work was boring. So I went and told my father that I wasn't
really enjoying myself. He looked at me for a moment, then
said, "That's why we call it 'work.'"

"But, Dad . . . it's hard and tiring and there's no way anyone
would want to do it." To which he replied, "That's why you get
paid." At age fifteen, that was what I needed to hear, but that attitude isn't adequate over a lifetime. Work isn't merely something to
endure, but neither is it the most important aspect of who we are.

What, then, is a proper theological understanding of work?
By work, I don't mean just our jobs; work is any act through
which we express or exert ourselves: gardening, cooking, teaching, construction, and on and on. Someone once asked
Sigmund Freud the secret of being happy. His answer was simple: "To love and to work." Working is essential for human
beings for several reasons: it brings us joy, it transforms us, and
it connects us to community.

Joy

Remember the film *Arthur*? Arthur, played by Dudley Moore,
is so rich, he can do anything. The problem is, he doesn't *have*

to do anything. He spends money as a form of entertainment. His days are spent in diversion, and as a consequence Arthur doesn't grow up. Only when his valet becomes deathly ill does Arthur discover the joy of work. He transforms Hobson's hospital room by bringing in his own furniture and organizes daily meals for his friend from the best restaurants in New York. Arthur is pulled out of himself and discovers the joy of being a co-creator.

There is joy in being transported by your work. It's the joy of the writer when the words flow through her, or the joy of an architect when he becomes so engrossed in a project that he stays up all night. Work is joyful because, when we are true to the task, we connect with our deepest self and with the world around us. As the poet Marge Piercy says, "But the thing worth doing well done / has a shape that satisfies, clean and evident."[3] That satisfaction of looking at a task and saying "I did that" is a joyous feeling. If we do not have it, then we and our world are diminished. It's why being chronically unemployed is a problem beyond economics: good work is a universal human need.

Transformation

On a basic level, the longer you work at something, the better you get at it. There was some point at which Yo Yo Ma could not play the cello. We learn certain skills through work, such as the abilities to concentrate and to be attentive. But the real transformation of work happens when we become completely engrossed in it and move into a different place. Artists say the Muse descends; sports figures say they get "in the zone." We become aware that we are connected to something outside of us that works through us.

The theological explanation of this is that the universe is not finished: our world is not static but organic. God's creation is

---

3. Marge Piercy, *Circles on the Water: Selected Poems of Marge Piercy* (New York: Knopf, 1986), 106.

not finished; instead, God is inviting us to participate in the transformation of the world. When we are at our best, we push creation a little further toward fulfillment.

When God created the world, God said, "It is good." When we create in our work, we hear echoes of that divine statement as well. When American poet Theodore Roethke wrote a poem he knew was right, he would weep for joy. Think about our world without Thomas Edison's light bulb or cars or penicillin or Mahler's Ninth Symphony. There would be less of the divine goodness in this world without them. Paul gets upset with those who refuse to work not because they are lazy, but because they are hindering what God is trying to do with God's world.

Connection

There is also another reason Paul is irritated with those who refuse to work: work connects us to community. Work is one of the ways we come in contact with the world and with others. Regardless of whether your work is being a lawyer or raising kids, there is always a communal aspect to it. For me, the best kind of work is with others, those moments when we find ourselves folded within a deeper rhythm and know the body of Christ for a moment. In fact, that is Paul's primary issue with the busybodies in Thessalonia. They don't recognize that their failure to work affects everyone else and gets in the way of what others are trying to do.

The truth is, we don't live for ourselves: what happens to you, affects me. Our work affects everyone, including those who come after us. In Nashville, we lived in a house built in 1924. Even though the pipes were old and the wiring was knob and tube, I loved that house because of the care someone took in its building. The ceiling in our bedroom closet was tongue and groove, the molding was gorgeous, and the banister was smooth and straight. Seventy years later, the work put into that house was still a delight. What will those who come after us think of our labors? When they look at our houses or our lives, what will they say?

Our work lifts all of humanity, and our failure to work denigrates it. Our work is not for ourselves but for God and what God is doing in the world. For that reason we work, but we don't work more than we should, or for our own glory. Joan Chittister writes that when she entered the convent she was shocked to learn that novices were forbidden to work during the day except at the prescribed hours. When she asked why, she was told that St. Benedict's Rule says, "Work while there is daylight." In other words, work balances prayer; it's part of what makes us whole, not the whole of what makes us whole.

So, where does all this leave us? First, we must embrace our work as a gift and not as an evil necessity. Beyond that, we must help create a world where people can find work that is real and good. Second, we must value what we do, knowing that God is in it whatever it is. Brother Lawrence, a seventeenth-century Carmelite mystic, saw even washing the dishes as a form of prayer. Instead of trying to get through our work, we should instead try to get into it. Finally, let us work for God and remember that our hands are the hands that God uses to transform the world.

Jean Vanier, the founder of the L'Arche community, says it best: "There is something very beautiful in work which is well and precisely done. It is a participation in the activity of God, who makes all things well and wisely, beautiful to the last detail."[4]

WOUNDS

Unless I see the mark of the nails in his hands, and put my finger in the mark of the nails and my hand in his side, I will not believe.

—John 20:25

4. Jean Vanier, *Community and Growth* (New York: Paulist Press, 1979), 194.

When I was five years old, I was . . . well, five years old. I acted like a five-year-old. It was the best of times, and it was the worst of times. There were a lot of best times—exploring the woods, playing baseball, spending time with my best friend, Bob—and there were a few worst times. I remember one worst time in particular.

It was before breakfast, and everyone was getting ready for school or work or kindergarten. My mother was kneeling on the kitchen floor looking for something in a cupboard, and I was trying to mix some grape juice. I took the frozen concentrate to the sink and stuck it under warm water, just like always. But as I was crossing the floor with the thawed syrup, something happened. One minute everything was fine, and the next minute the grape juice was flying through the air onto my mother's head. In a single moment, my mother turned into a purple demon.

I tore out of the kitchen and hid behind the couch, certain that I had cut myself off from those that I loved. I knew in my five-year-old heart that I was simply beyond redemption. Even if my mother could find me, even if there were any way she could say the magic words that she forgave me, it wouldn't do any good: I knew what I had done, and I knew who I was. It was like that old Groucho Marx joke: I wouldn't want to join any club that would have me as a member. That deep shame blocked my five-year-old self from thinking that there was any place for me in the circle of life.

I tell this story not to document my own inherent sinfulness, but to help us engage the story of Thomas's encounter with the risen Christ. John writes that the disciples were meeting together after Jesus' death, and that they had locked the door. John says they were afraid of "the Jews"—but maybe there's another reason for the locked door.

We know that Mary Magdalene had told them what she saw; we know that John and Peter saw the empty tomb; we know they had heard the stories about Jesus coming back from the dead. So, maybe they locked the door in an effort to hide behind the couch. After all, they all had fallen asleep in the garden and run from the soldiers. Peter—the Rock—denied the Lord three times. Maybe in their hearts they thought, "Even if he has come back, what would he have to do with me?"

Jesus comes among them at this point and again a week later when Thomas is there. Both times, he does two things. First, he says, "Peace be with you"—that is, *Shalom*, or "Wholeness be with you." Jesus pronounces the peace that passes all understanding, the peace that comes when we know that God is with us. He pronounces that God's love drives away all our fears. Second, Jesus shows the disciples his wounds—which is very strange, when you think about it. Why does the risen Christ have wounds, anyway? No other gospel account mentions them. Mary Magdalene grabs Jesus' feet, but she doesn't say anything about wounds. The disciples on the road to Emmaus break bread with him, but they don't mention any nail holes. Why the wounds?

The interesting part about this is that the disciples do not recognize Jesus until they see his wounds. John says, "He showed them his hands and his side. *Then* the disciples rejoiced when they saw the Lord" (John 20:20). Later, John says that it is when Jesus shows his hands to Thomas that Thomas says, "My Lord and my God!" (John 20:28).

One reason the disciples know Jesus by his wounds is that our wounds or our scars are a physical record of our past. I still have a scar on my left arm from when I stuck my hand through a window at the age of four. When we touch our scars, we touch our past. In Homer's epic tale, Odysseus comes home after twenty years, disguised as an old man. No one recognizes him except the nurse, who sees a scar on his leg while bathing him. She remembers when he got that scar as a boy and reattaches his history to him.

The disciples want to know if this risen Christ—the one who can walk through doors—is connected to the Jesus they knew. We want to know that, as well. What does our experience of peace, of wholeness, have to do with Jesus of Nazareth, who lived two thousand years ago? Can we touch the scars? Can we recognize Jesus in the midst of our experience? To do so, we have to know what the nurse knew and what the disciples knew: we have to know the story. In American Sign Language, the sign "Jesus" is created by placing the index finger of each hand in the palm of the other. Jesus is the one with wounded hands.

There is also a deeper reason why the disciples are interested in the wounds, why Thomas says, "Unless I see the mark of the nails in his hands . . . I will not believe" (John 20:25). The disciples, like us, want to see Jesus' wounds to know that he is connected to our wounds. What good does a resurrected Christ do us if he abandons us in our pain? The disciples know that they are wounded and are well aware of their own shortcomings and failures. They want to know if Jesus left them behind when he rose from the dead. Their question is not, "Was he raised?" but "Are we alone?"

Resurrection is about life on the other side of death. On this side of death, we are always splitting the world in two: good and bad, joy and pain. On the other side, we find *shalom* or wholeness, and God is in all of it. The risen Christ has nail holes in his hands but still gathers up all that we have and all that we are and blesses it.

Resurrection is not about escaping suffering but about having all of our life redeemed. We touch his wounds to our wounds so that we die with him and are raised with him. The risen Christ has not come to take away our wounds—he has come to take away our fear. Thomas touched Jesus' wounds and knew that Jesus was still part of his life. Even though Thomas ran away, even though Thomas wasn't there the first time, Jesus appeared.

I heard of a woman named Sally who lost her job, her family, and her health to alcoholism. Sally knew she was wounded. She believed in God, but she did not believe that God could love someone like her. Then, one night Sally dreamed that she was lying in bed, and Jesus came and stood before her with his arms open wide in a blessing. Sally looked at Jesus and said,

"Why have you come to me? Why *me*?" Jesus replied, "Because that's who I am."

When you find yourself hiding behind the couch or locked in a room for fear, make the sign for Jesus. Put your fingers in the palm of your hands. Touch the wounds. Feel the holes. Know that the risen Christ touches your wounds—because that's who he is.

X ("X" IS THE GREEK LETTER THAT BEGINS THE WORD "CHRIST")

"Lord, to whom can we go? You have the words of eternal life."

—John 6:68

When Jesus spoke about eating his flesh and drinking his blood, his words were difficult for his Jewish audience. As a matter of fact, John's gospel says that because of Jesus' teaching, "many . . . turned back and no longer went about with him" (6:66). As they leave, Jesus turns to the Twelve and asks, "Do you also wish to go away?" Simon Peter answers, "Lord, to whom can we go? You have the words of eternal life."

I used to teach English in a college that was affiliated with the Southern Baptists. Once, as I advised a student about her schedule, I asked her if she came to this college because she was a Baptist. She said, "Oh, I'm not a Christian. I'm a musician."

Sometimes we act as if faith in Jesus Christ is an extracurricular activity. We act as if all the possible diversionary activities are spread out before us: there's sports and there's community service and there's fun things like movies and concerts and, oh, yes, there's also Jesus Christ.

Sometimes we are so presumptuous, as if faith in our Lord is a matter of taste or as if our connection to him is of relative importance. A consumer mentality pervades everything we do. Therefore, we decide whether we can fit Jesus Christ into our busy schedules. We decide whether we "agree" with the gospel and can affirm its principles. We act as if we should take a poll to decide if Jesus is really the Christ.

In an interview, novelist Walker Percy was once asked how belief in the dogma of the Catholic Church was possible in this day and age. "What else is there?" he replied. The interviewer said, "What do you mean what else is there? There is humanism, atheism, agnosticism, Marxism, behaviorism, materialism, Buddhism, Mohammedanism, Sufism, astrology, occultism, theosophy." To which Percy replied, "That's what I mean."[1]

In an affluent culture like ours, our luxuries and our degree of autonomy can give us the illusion that we don't need the gospel of Jesus Christ for life itself. Often the discovery of our need is a shock.

To be fair, I admit that there are many ways that people come to their senses and have a conversion. Wonderful events can occur that enable people to recognize the presence of grace in their lives. However, my guess is that for most of us in our culture, we have to be *jolted* out of the illusion that we are self-sufficient. My guess is that most of us have to hit a brick wall before we can realize that we are not at the center of the universe or before we realize that life doesn't always work out in the ways we desire. Sometimes, we have to come to that brick wall before we can discover where we belong.

It's always hard for us. It goes against our grain. We don't *like* to need anyone else. We don't *like* belonging to someone else. We don't *like* being wholly dependent on someone else.

---

1. Walker Percy, *Conversations with Walker Percy* (Jackson: University of Mississippi, 1985), 175.

Therefore, we surround ourselves with precisely what we don't need and neglect the one person we do need.

Dan Wakefield has written an autobiography called *Returning*. This book describes his discovery of how lost he was. It begins like this: "One balmy spring morning in Hollywood, a month or so before my forty-eighth birthday, I woke up screaming. I got out of bed, went into the next room, sat down on a couch, and screamed again."[2]

That balmy spring morning, Dan Wakefield's life fell apart. All the comfortable compromises he had made with himself no longer worked. All those careful ways of coping no longer served. Dan Wakefield discovered that he could no longer keep going in the same direction. He had no choice; he had to rediscover what finally matters. Therefore, he returned to a life of sobriety. He returned to his home in Boston. And he returned to his faith.

I cannot speak for everyone, but for me, faith comes when you know that there is a hole in your heart that only Jesus Christ can fill. When I read the gospels, I see the people who come to Jesus have nowhere else to go. They are not the "looking good" folks. They are not the people who are in control, because those people don't need a savior. They believe they can save themselves. Those people don't need eternal life; they believe they have created their own life.

"Do you wish to go away?" "Lord, to whom can we go? You have the words of eternal life." The people who come to Jesus have no illusions about what they need. They know that there is no gadget or job or addiction or leisure activity that can fill the hole in their hearts.

Luke tells us of a woman who has been hemorrhaging for twelve years. She has spent all her money on physicians. There is no cure. As Jesus is walking by, she comes up behind him to touch the fringe of his cloak. *Lord, to whom can we go?* Or the prostitute who is so desperate she breaks into a banquet and

---

2. Dan Wakefield, *Returning: A Spiritual Journey* (New York: Doubleday, 1988), 3.

grabs Jesus' feet and bathes them with her tears. *Lord, to whom can we go?*

I know that many people see faith in Christ as one option among many, but for me, it's life or death. That's not because I am a holy person. It's not because God has given me any mystical experience. And it's certainly not because I have intellectually decided that Christianity makes sense.

It's because I have nowhere else to go. Jesus Christ gives me life—eternal life that is right now. Jesus Christ is not something we fit into our lives. He is not one more activity. Our connection to him is at the center of who we are.

"Do you wish to go away?"

"Lord, to whom can we go?"

YES

I will put my law within them, and I will write it on
their hearts; and I will be their God, and they shall be
my people.

—Jeremiah 31:33

Jeremiah had a double vision, that is, he had two things to say.
Unfortunately, because the Southern Kingdom, Judah, would
not hear the first thing, they could not hear the second. That's
the way it is with prophets, but because they are prophets, their
messages are preserved a long time. Let's see if we can do any
better than Judah.

The first thing had to do with the bad times that were and
the worse times that were coming. People didn't want to hear
about bad times just then, because the king of Assyria, Judah's
ancient enemy, had died, and people were starting to relax.

Jeremiah, however, could not relax, because he wasn't looking southward toward Assyria, he was looking northward to
Babylonia, where he could see the Babylonians gathering at the
border. After telling Jeremiah that Babylonia would conquer

Judah and the Jews would be thrown into a long, alienating exile, God sent Jeremiah to tell the news that no one wanted to hear. He told the people of Judah that bad times were coming; bad times were here. He told them that the Babylonians would sack Jerusalem and all that they held dear would be lost: their homes, their Temple, their land.

The people of Judah reacted to this news by throwing Jeremiah in prison and turning a blind eye to the reality that surrounded them, but their ignorance and denial did not stop the future from coming. Soon, Jerusalem was sacked, the Temple was destroyed, and the Jews were sent into exile.

We are often like the Israelites: as Richard Rohr says, we want consolation without confrontation. I have a friend who is a therapist, and he says that all his clients want to feel better, but they don't want to change. Jeremiah reminds us that we cannot pretend our problems away. Whether we like it or not, we are facing exile, and the sooner we are honest about our condition, the sooner we can move to where God is calling us to be. Half of the prophet's call is for faithful people to take a good hard look at where they are and where they are going.

Jesus has a similar message. He tells the disciples, "Whoever serves me must follow me"—and the path he gives them is to lose their life in this world in order to discover eternal life. In other words, we cannot pretend that the order in which we live is God's will. We cannot pretend that the Babylonians aren't upon us. We cannot pretend that the way things are is the way they ought to be. God intends that we weep over our profound displacement. God intends that we feel our exile.

In the film *Good Will Hunting*, the main character is a young man who has exiled himself from his true talents and vocation—although he is a mathematical genius, he works as a janitor at MIT. He is stuck in a world that is never home to him, stuck with a life that doesn't fit. Instead of living a life of the mind, he goes to bars and gets into fights. Finally, a psychologist helps him confront his deep sense of loss and exile. The therapist repeats "It's not your fault" over and over again, until the tears of loss and pain and regret run down Will's face. Only then is he able to move and change. First he must feel the grief and be confronted with his dislocation. Only then can he be consoled.

Jeremiah's invitation is also Jesus' invitation. What in this world, what in this system do we need to confess as being profoundly deadly? From which aspects of the way we live do we need to extricate ourselves? What are the forces that place us in exile? The invitation is to stop accommodating ourselves to Babylon and to name the destroyer for what it is.

That invitation is half of Jeremiah's message and half of the good news of Jesus. If we can hear that half, then we can receive the other half: to remember the promise. Jeremiah tells the people that God has promised to make a new covenant that will not be like the old covenant: "I will put my law within them, and I will write it on their hearts; and I will be their God, and they shall be my people." After confession comes consolation, the consolation that God promises new life after exile.

The NRSV translates verse six in Psalm 51 this way: "You desire truth in the inward being." God longs for us to come home, to stop living in the kingdom of death and move toward the kingdom of life. The vision that God gives Jeremiah is that one day our will and God's will be one. It's a vision of a time when we will not have to struggle and fret over what God wants us to do but will know it intuitively. God's law will be in our hearts, and not only will our external exile end, our internal exile will end as well.

Just before his death, Thomas Merton wrote, "God places in my heart a 'yes' to Him. . . . My destiny in life . . . is to uncover this 'yes' so that my life is totally and completely a 'yes' to God, a complete assent to God."[1] The promise is that our "yes" deep in our hearts will fill our lives, and every act we take, every word we utter, will be in accord with God's will. We pray "Thy will be done on earth"—the promise is that, one day, it will be.

---

1. Thomas Merton, *Thomas Merton in Alaska* (New York: New Direction, 1988), 154.

We know that the people of Judah could not hear Jeremiah's double vision—confrontation followed by consolation. Can we? In 1980, Jimmy Carter ran for president against Ronald Reagan. In the previous year, Carter had given a speech in which he pronounced that there was a "malaise" in the United States. That declaration came back to haunt him during the presidential campaign. Capitalizing on the reaction to that speech, Reagan's campaign slogan was: "It's morning again in America." It is no coincidence that Reagan won. The campaign presented these two messages as a choice: malaise or morning. It's not a hard choice, but it's a false choice.

The truth is, we must choose both malaise and morning, both confrontation and consolation. We must confess and grieve over what ails us while we look for the promise. To do otherwise is to be either cynical or dangerously naïve. God invites us to be honest about where we are, yet to live in expectation of where we are going.

Perhaps Jeremiah gives us a clear sense of how to accept this invitation. As we have seen, he had spouted off one too many times about the bad times ahead and was thrown into prison. The Babylonians attacked Jerusalem while Jeremiah was in prison. They had already captured the area to the north of the city, including Jeremiah's hometown of Anathoth. After the attack, when Jeremiah was free again, there was no food in the city, and people were so hungry that they resorted to cannibalism. Jeremiah knew how bad things were, but he also remembered God's promises. He bought a piece of property: a field in Anathoth, even though the Babylonians were in control of that territory. He invested in the promise in the midst of the malaise.

When you and I are honest about all that plagues our lives and our world, we don't have to be told that the kingdom is not yet here. Let's be honest about our sin and confess our parts in it, but let's also remember that God has promised a new covenant—a time when the law of our hearts will be the law of the Lord—and invest in the promise. Let's look for those places in our lives and in our world that have been overtaken by Babylon and invest ourselves in them, even if the voices in our heads say "that will never work."

In fact, the new covenant is here and the law is in our hearts—we just need to listen to what God is calling for us to do. We just need to pay attention to that still, small voice within that is our "yes," and then act. We just need to buy a field.

Z

ZION

When the LORD restored the fortunes of Zion, we were like those who dream.

—Psalm 126:1

When I was twelve years old, my family took a vacation to a ranch in Florida about forty minutes from Gainesville. Perhaps "ranch" isn't the right word. It was a farmhouse my cousins loaned to us on fifty acres with a pond and four horses.

We got there one June morning and unpacked and explored before lunch. That afternoon, my brother and my sister and I pestered our parents to let us ride the horses. They sort of plodded along a well-worn trail, but to me it was the Wild West.

We came back to the farmhouse just as my Dad was getting up from his nap. He came out to the porch and waved to us as we rode into sight of the house. Just as he was turning to go back in, I saw him flinch and grab his neck. By the time we put the horses in the barn and walked toward the house, I knew something was wrong.

My mother was screaming for us to get in the car. My father had been stung by a yellow jacket on the vein running down his neck and had gone into shock. My brother and I carried him to the back of the station wagon and we took off to Gainesville.

At twelve, I didn't know what to do. I couldn't open his mouth. I tried giving him artificial respiration through his nose, but I didn't know if that helped or hurt. I just prayed over and over again, "Please let him be okay. Please let him be okay."

For a long time we didn't know if he really would be okay. His blood pressure dropped off the chart during the ride. We sat in the waiting room, not really saying anything, just staring into space. It felt as if our lives were over. It felt as if we had fallen through some trapdoor during an innocent walk across the stage, and we had no idea how to get back.

After a long, long wait, the doctor came and told us our Dad was going to be fine—

When the Lord restored the fortunes of Zion,
    we were like those who dream.
Then our mouth was filled with laughter,
    and our tongue with shouts of joy. . . .
May those who sow in tears
    reap with shouts of joy.
(Psalm 126:1–2, 5)

Zion is the vision of wholeness and home. Zion is the dream of all that has been lost and promised to be restored. During the ride to the hospital, I did not think I would have a father. Suddenly my life was given back to me. In that moment of reversal, anything was possible. If he could come back to life, we could dream dreams we had been too timid to dream. The future suddenly opened to me. Zion had come near.

When all that was lost was returned, it was returned seven-fold because I knew, at least in my twelve-year-old way, what mattered and what didn't. I didn't want to ride a horse. I wanted my father to be alive.

God does not invite us to dream "of a white Christmas just like the ones I used to know." God invites us to dream of a world that has never been but has always been promised. God invites us to open our arms and eyes and hearts to the blessings God gives us. As we give thanks, we realize that anything is possible.

The truth is that we live in an enchanted world. In Isaiah 65:17, God proclaims, "I am about to create new heavens and a new earth." As God gives us back more than what was lost, God invites us to dream joyous dreams, outlandish dreams.

God's invitation is to be like Jacob, or any of the great dreamers of scripture, and to dream of a ladder connecting heaven and earth. In Advent, we think about the Word becoming flesh. The astonishment of that event, the sheer surprise of that wonderful happening, opens us up to dream wild dreams. We are free to dream of a world that looks the way God intends the world to look. In Advent, we are invited to open our imaginations and to step outside our little status quo boxes and to dream bigger, to dream wider and wilder.

What is God's dream for us? What is the dream that God invites us to share? Again in Isaiah, God tells us: "They shall build houses and inhabit them; they shall plant vineyards and eat their fruit. . . . My chosen shall long enjoy the work of their hands" (65:21, 22).

The word for this is "fecundity." In God's world, each person will live out his or her true vocation. What we do will be an extension of who we are. How many people dread going to work? How many people can say that they are truly connected to what they do? Work is too often only a means to an end. God's dream is that all persons be fecund—be fruitful—have a part to play. Psychologist Rollo May once said that people will express themselves one way or another. If they cannot do so constructively, they will do so destructively. God's dream is that all people find a place in building up the kingdom through using their gifts.

In Isaiah God also says, "No more shall there be in [Jerusalem] an infant that lives but a few days, or an old person who does not live out a lifetime" (Isaiah 65:20). Life is the most precious gift we have. It's the first gift given to us by God. We are to cherish it and nurture it and protect it. Of course, accidents happen. Of course, tragedies occur. However, these are not God's intention. Let us dream of a world in which all life is precious—not just here in the affluent United States but in Rwanda and Bosnia and the Sudan. Let us dream of a world where people do not die by the thousands of simple starvation. Let us dream of a world where the infant mortality of the West becomes the norm for the world. Let us dream of a world where all people share in the amazing medical discoveries of our century. Or of a world where there are not so many senseless deaths from shootings in schools. Read the paper and ask yourself if this is God's dream.

Finally, Isaiah reminds us that God's dream is where "The wolf and the lamb shall feed together.... They shall not hurt or destroy on all my holy mountain" (Isaiah 65:25). God's dream is a dream of peace—of *shalom*—of all people living in harmony. We all know how far away we are from that dream. We know how many categories we can use to divide ourselves from one another.

Advent is a time to cleanse our vision so that we do not see the divisions and so that we do not accept the divisions. Advent is the time when we give up our resignation. We stop saying "That's the way it is."

Instead we dare to dream as God dreams. We dream of a world of connections and not divisions. We dream of a world where might doesn't make right; right makes right. We dream of a world where "all God's children, black [people] and white [people], Jews and Gentiles, Protestants and Catholics, will be able to join hands and sing in the words of the old ... spiritual: Free at last ... thank God Almighty we are free at last!"[1]

---

1. Martin Luther King Jr., "I Have a Dream," speech delivered on the steps at the Lincoln Memorial in Washington, DC, on August 28, 1963.

In the bleak midwinter, when the dark descends earlier and earlier, in a time when the sheer routine of preparing for the holy day seems less and less magical and more and more of a chore—cards to send, presents to buy, parties to attend—we need to stop for a moment and reflect upon the gift that lies waiting to be discovered. Just when we were certain that our way was lost for good, just when we thought that our world was over, God gives us life. God comes among us and restores all that was broken. God leads us out of exile back to Zion.

In the face of that goodness and grace, may we dream again. May we dream of the world God dreams of: a world where people have work that is who they are; a world in which all life is precious; a world of *shalom*.

After the doctor came and told us the news of our father, my brother, sister, mother, and I looked at ourselves. My sister had no shoes on. My brother and I had on old Asheville High football jerseys, and my mother had forgotten her wallet and had no money or identification. As we realized all that had happened, we made the only appropriate response—we laughed and we laughed and we laughed, because we knew Zion must be near.